LEAN into it
A Journey of Continuous Improvement

Hahn, Lucas

Contents

Why Not LEAN into life?

A Lean Journey of Continuous Improvement In:
Work, Personal Growth, Health, The Home, Sports, and Religion

Lean Continuous Improvement is a profound, valuable, inspirational, and impactful way of life. It begins and ends with Respect for People and has become as important to me as air, food, and water. I can't do without it. On my own improvement journey, I have had many learning moments and have struggled to understand why everyone is not doing this? I have learned that there are key components missing in most implementations.

This book reveals secrets closely guarded by the successful, secrets that constitute their competitive edge. I aim to democratize this advantage, empowering every reader to achieve similar success.

If you have been on an improvement journey that has fallen short of your expectations the same roadmap can help you understand where the missteps were so you can go back and get on the right path. Lean absolutely, positively needs to be done with people, not to them! This book will unlock some of those secrets that the successful don't want you to know. This is their competitive advantage and I want to bring everyone forward.

The Journey Begins

LEAN EVERYTHING

PREFACE

Why Me? There are lots of experts out there, so why listen to me? I have researched and learned from many sources and have been applying this mentality for most of my life. This has been a journey and I am very passionate about sharing that journey with the intent to inspire others and grow a culture of respecting everyone and continuously improving.

Where I am. I have had high aspirations for myself for as long as I could remember. I absolutely hated to lose, I hated to not be good at things, I hated to not have what I wanted, I hated that I wasn't a natural athlete or born into financial wealth, but I loved working. Not just working but working hard and getting better; getting better at sports, at my profession, at home, at building and construction and eventually, at being a husband, a Dad, and helping my community, family and friends. Now, getting better at absolutely everything. As I reflect on that hatred turning into a strong passion and love for improvement I recognize a lot of contributing factors, my caring for others, my ambition and drive, my work ethic, my friends, family and community, my desire to learn and perhaps the most important and impactful thing, my introduction to Lean, Six Sigma Continuous Improvement.

So, where do I stand on those things I hated and the thing I loved? I feel very awkward saying this, because it doesn't feel like the typical 'me', but I am proud of where I am. I no longer hate where I stand on any of those things. I am at a position beyond any expectations I had for myself on any of those topics. Furthermore, and perhaps the most exciting thing is I know I am nowhere near done. I know there is a ton of room for growth in everything I do and plan to do. So why is that? Again, lots of contributing factors, and perhaps the most important and impactful, my passion and desire for Lean Continuous Improvement.

With all the amazing things Lean has done and currently does for me, I need to share that story and hopefully it has a similar impact on others. I had a great Lean mentor and person I hold in very high regard tell me once; while trying to talk me off the Lean ledge, as long as one person got something out of what he was teaching or coaching it was worth it. I completely agree with his statement and would certainly be happy if the sharing of my story has a profound and valuable impact on one person, but I am not accepting that. I need this impact to go way beyond that. I prefer to see my positive impacts increase through multiplication, others learning and acting this way in a manner that is inspiring to others, thus multiplying the impacts. I not only want this to reach and help a lot of folks, but I want them to be inspired to share their achievements, impacts and journey to help others.

A little note for you on the construct of this book. After Chapter 5 the chapters do not necessarily build on each other, so feel free to jump into the chapters you think will bring you value. I do hope there is something valuable for you in each chapter, but if you have no interest in sports for example, feel free to skip that chapter. Don't skip Chapter 14, you will break my heart. Another note about the book. I am a complete sponge for knowledge on improvement, Lean and otherwise, so I am constantly reading. As I read books that might have been recommended or I stumble across, I usually find references within to other books and find myself building a wish list of books to consume next. There is a list of books that provided positive impacts for me on Lean, Leadership or Continuous Improvement at the end of this book. There is also a brief write up on each. So, if you are a learning sponge like me, don't miss that part.

SOME KEY ELEMENTS
AND BACKGROUND
OF LEAN

To me, Lean is a mentality of reducing or eliminating waste or struggles by engaging and inspiring everyone to respect people and continuously improve.

———

L et me start by saying if you have a strong background in Lean Six Sigma, you may get to the end of this chapter and feel like you spent a couple of minutes for nothing, so feel free to skip Chapter 1. I am intending this Chapter to give some real high-level information on Lean and Six Sigma for the novice or folks who aren't sure what they are being told Lean is, is accurate. There is a lot of fake lean out there. If it is not continuous and starting with respect for people, it is not lean. I am also going to touch on why this book will not speak to the six-sigma piece much after this section. The focus will be on Lean principles, behaviors and tools.

With that clarification out of the way I am ready to share my understanding and perspective and some historical facts on what Lean Six Sigma Continuous Improvement is. Most believe Lean started in Japan at Toyota in the 1950's, providing me with a nice opportunity to explain the two leaders quoted on the prior pages. As well as what is broadly known as the two Pillars of Lean, Respect for People and Continuous Improvement.

First, and first for a reason is Dr. Shigeo Shingo. Dr. Shingo is and industrial engineer from Japan who made many contributions to improving industry and manufacturing in Japan, including key contributions to Toyota and the Toyota Production System. The Shingo Institute at Utah State and coveted Shingo Prize are all named after him. He is first because his focus was on people and their behaviors, which add up to the culture. You can consider this the Lean side of the Lean Six Sigma mantra and where this book will focus. That is not to say Dr. Deming did not have a people focus, Shingo was just on another level.

I whole heartedly believe Respect for People is the most critical pillar of Lean. If this pillar is not a focus and doesn't have a sound foundation, receiving regular attention and support, all other efforts will fall short of what they could achieve. People that are disrespected or feel disrespected are not engaged, motivated or inspired to make meaningful, sustainable, improvements. You can roll out the coolest tools in the world, but they will achieve no results or inferior results if the teams utilizing those tools have no desire to improve and achieve better results.

The Shingo Model and Shingo Institute is alive and thriving today. The Model and the Institute continue to have a major impact on business cultures all around the world. If you are not familiar with the Shingo Model or Institute I would encourage you to fire up your favorite search engine and do some poking around, extremely impactful and energizing stuff. I have taken the steps to become Shingo certified and it has been one of the most rewarding, impactful and enjoyable things I have done. It starts with a focus on ideal behaviors producing ideal results, all aligned with your business goals and mission. Now on to the other part of this dynamic duo.

Dr. W. Edwards Deming is a brilliant American Engineer and statistician who also had a major impact on industry and manufacturing in Japan. He brought impactful, data driven tools and philosophies to the table drastically changing the way things are manufactured, how problems are solved and how people engage in their work. You can think of this as the Six Sigma side of the Lean Six Sigma mantra. Please keep in mind they overlap and are dependent on each other to obtain success. I will not focus much on the six sigma, the complex data and tools piece as I move forward. The tools and philosophies he innovated put much needed structure to the vast amount of energy beginning to bubble up at Toyota. Deming is also well known for his 14 Points on Total Quality Management.

I saw this need on my own journey and continue to see this need in my world. Once this way of life begins to take hold of you the energy, excitement and passion can get out of control quickly. You see improvement opportunities everywhere and it is almost maddening to wrap your brain around it all. Therefore, the structure and rigor Dr. Deming brings to the table very quickly becomes mandatory to manage your sanity. I continue to find myself having to grab more structure from time to time to reign me back in. I hope you all find the same problem, it is a great problem to have.

So why all this Toyota business? From when these two great innovators, among others, started to have an impact on shifting the culture at Toyota; post World War II, as a rebuilding effort, until the late 1970's this Japanese automobile manufacturer moved from an afterthought and insignificant contributor to the world and more importantly the U.S.

automotive market to one of the greats. They were producing affordable products with a focus on quality. It became very difficult for the major U.S. auto manufacturers to keep up with the quality, performance, cost and overall value of a Toyota product. It is pretty amazing to think about, when you consider the vast resources, substantial head start, government support and cultural advantages the Big 3, GM, Ford and Chrysler had at the time. Americans in the 1970's wanted to buy American and didn't want to buy Japanese. However, the value gap started to become too great and buyer sentiment began to shift.

There are many books by many authors, as well as courses and videos out there on Toyota and the Toyota Production System (TPS). I encourage you to seek those out and learn from them. There is a lot of great stuff out there and I use much of it every day. I will highlight one key learning opportunity, Jim Womack's 1990 book, improved in 2007, "The Machine That Changed the World". This amazing book is recognized as a key development that blew the lid off the jar and gave everyone a peek at the impressive improvement culture at Toyota. It provides others with the ingredients to start to close the culture Gap. I will forewarn the book is very heavy and technical around automobile manufacturing. The impacts and mass amount of change is what jumped out to me, as I don't manufacture automobiles.

The thing about closing the Gap is this; the Lean Six Sigma business mentality is so engrained in Toyota, the target keeps moving forward. Toyota today is better than Toyota yesterday and substantially better than Toyota decades ago. Putting the full embodiment of Continuous Improvement on display. Here is a key thing I learned on my Lean Journey, specifically as it relates to bringing others along. Toyota is an absolutely necessary part of the story, but it also can become a hindrance.

As I attempted to bring teams along in an industry that does not manufacture anything, it became a hurdle, and an excuse used by people who resist change, or who are too busy to change or just flat out have bad habits. I can't tell you how many times I heard, *"we don't manufacture anything, or we don't make cars, or we don't make widgets; this doesn't apply to us."* Well guess what, it does! The story of my Journey will prove to you that this powerful mentality applies to everything.

As I press forward with my writing and you all press forward with your lean journey, I think it is important to keep the Lean timeline shown below.

Lean Timeline

1950's – Toyota Started Seeing Value
(20 Years)
1970"s – Toyota Competes in the U.S. Market
(20 + Years)
1990 – Womack helps others crack the code, and quickly lots of manufacturing, automotive and others start to leverage Lean
(11 years)
2001 – You start to see it in Health Care (Virginia Mason)
(10 Years)
2011 – You start to see Lean Continuous Improvement in Government, Sports, Law Firms, Education and other non-manufacturing environments
(2 Years)
2013 – I get hit right in the face with it. My Lean Journey starts in earnest
(10 Years)
2023 – I am so passionate and engaged in this Lean Journey I can't help but share it

———

As I have learned and the timeline shows, this is a journey. There is no silver bullet or magic wand, it takes time, focus and effort and is so worth it. My journey is not a straight line, it does not go from start directly upward toward a goal. It goes up, then down, then up and so on. This is how my journey has gone and continues to go. This is also how the journey of many others has gone and continues to go.

In physics you hear the phrase, what goes up must go down. As it relates to my Lean journey things are a little different, what goes down, must go up. That is continuous improvement. Those, downs provide valuable experience, impactful lessons and are ripe with opportunities for improvement. They are a very necessary part of the journey and can sometimes be difficult to overcome. Make sure you have a support system, surround yourself with others that get it and use them as a sound board and motivation. I have been truly blessed with a wonderful network of support and truly appreciate them all.

I will now share, at a very high level some of the tools, principles and behaviors you may find not only valuable, but key parts of a Lean culture displaying continuous improvement. You will notice many of them are designated with Japanese words, due to the Toyota influence. Perhaps a term you will hear almost everywhere is Kaizen, which means improvement. You will hear folks talk about Kaizen events or Kaizen boards. This all centered around the idea that improvements are necessary and never ending.

You will also hear the Japanese word Kanban, which is a visual system intended to drive desired behaviors. There are lots of great examples of Kanban out there and most use colors or lights or other clear and intuitive indicators to drive certain behaviors. For example, a Red card intentionally inserted into a supply, like paper or cleaning supplies at the point when things should be re-ordered.

Along the same lines and very similar are visual management tools. This can be any visual management out there driving desired behavior, or stifling un-desired behavior. I can go on for hours just about Visual Management and how impactful it has been to me. I will get much deeper into this further along in the book. A good example of impactful, simple visual management is a smiley face sticker or gold star someone might receive for doing a good job or achieving a goal.

I put some depth to some of these major categories as they are critical and highly leveraged in Lean Communities. However, I don't want this book to turn into a textbook or massive piece of reference material, so I am going to list out other Lean principles, tools and behaviors with a simple explanation. There are lots of great resources out there you can engage with to learn more. I will also be pointing out in the following chapters if one of these are being applied to the topic at hand.

SOME LEAN TERMS AND DEFINITIONS

5S – Steps to follow in this order: Sort, Set in Order, Shine, Standardize, Sustain

Poka Yoke – Mistake Proofing, engineer out the chance to make a mistake

Standard Work – Clear documentation on how to execute work, the who, how, where and when can all be part of standard work. Generates predicable, repeatable results.

Process Mapping – Visualization of the steps in a process, made available at point of use for workers to use as a structure to produce consistent results and visually identify opportunities for improvement. A great way to show how many complex steps in a processes are connected and dependent on each other.

Structured Problem Solving – There are several Methods out there, PDCA(Plan-Do-Check-Adjust), OODA (Observe-Orient-Decide-Act), DMAIC (Define-Measure-Analyze-Improve-Control), 8 Step/A3 (1.Clarify and Validate Problem 2. Identify Gaps 3. Set Improvement Targets 4. Root Cause Analysis 5. Develop Countermeasures 6. See Countermeasures through 7. Confirm Results 8. Standardize

Rapid Improvement Event (RIE) – A very structured way of getting everyone that does the work in a room to solve problems. Don't let the name fool you, if you don't have sound, documented processes and good metrics to define your problem the pre-work needed for these to be successful can be anything but Rapid. Once you are ready, this process is highly effective at quickly closing a gap and producing sustainable improvements.

Gemba Walks – (Japanese for actual place) A structured, defined way for leaders to engage where the work happens to remove hurdles and identify empowerment gaps from the front lines.

Voice of the Customer – A customer is something or someone who consumes all or part of something you produce. The Voice of that is extremely important. This can be an internal downstream customer or external customer. You MUST know if you are meeting their needs from cost, quality, time or any combination of these.

Visual Management – A clear, intuitive tool that provide visual information to drive desired behavior, or discourage undesired behavior.

Value Stream – these are the tasks, steps or activities that add value for the customer. Visualizing this is very powerful and is referred to as Value Stream Mapping

Root Cause Analysis – Getting to the Root Cause of a problem, there are several methods, 5 Why's, Fishbone Diagram, and Fault Tree Diagram are some popular ones.

Lean Countermeasure – This is something that reduces or eliminates a Gap determined in your Root Cause Analysis. The Lean mind is always looking to insert a countermeasure as early in a process as possible. This is where the effort is typically smaller and the impact larger.

Waste – Anything that does not bring Value to the customer. Something they would not pay for separately. Typically broken up into 8 types: Defects Overproduction Waiting Non-Utilized Potential Transportation Inventory Motion Extra Processing

Flow – removing waste to make the process more efficient

Pull – the next step is pulling the product or information down the process, as opposed to it being pushed, which can generate a lot of waste.

System Aim – an aim that ensures everybody in the entire system wins. Must be clear and managed.

KBI – Key Behavior Indicator, a measurement of the behaviors that are producing the results, there are a type of leading indicator.

Now that we got some of the pure academics of lean behind us, I want to provide some thoughts on non-manufacturing examples of Lean Continuous Improvement.

There is a lot of great information out there on Virginia Mason, a highly successful healthcare network in the Pacific Northwest actively living a very stout and mature Lean Culture. There is a Virginia Mason Institute that is a key Lean Resource for organizations around the world. You will find books like "Transforming Health Care", by Charles Kenney and "Accelerating Health Care Transformation with Lean and Innovation", by Paul Plsek, among many others out there telling the story of Virginia Mason and the Impacts they are getting and having by shifting to a Lean Culture. There is a lot of information out there proving amazing insight to how this Health Care provider took this manufacturing born business mentality and provided incredible value and amazing results in a very non-manufacturing environment.

As I reflect on the other non-manufacturing environments flourishing with a Lean culture, I simply must talk about the New Zealand All Blacks Rugby team. The book, "Legacy" by James Kerr is a great read and highlights the culture of the winningest Professional Sports franchise in the world. They have been winning for decades. The wins don't come by chance, they come on purpose and are a direct result of their culture. A culture steeped in strong traditions and a focus on continuous improvement.

There are lots of other places in Sports where I see Lean Continuous Improvement on display, but not a lot of references or public material out there sharing how Lean Continuous Improvement is helping them not only win but develop a sustainable culture of winning. I can only imagine in the big business and ruthlessly competitive environment of professional sports folks are not real eager to be the "Womack", the bean spiller, and share the secrets to success. As far as I know, you will not find a ton of literature out there beyond, "Legacy", but as you learn to adopt Lean you will see signs of it everywhere, especially in professional sport.

Perhaps one of the best resources to identify other, non-manufacturing applications of Lean you can explore is with someone that started and continues to work in the manufacturing space but takes a Lean approach to everything. A major contributor to my Lean success and journey is Paul Akers. He has many resources available, and I encourage you to explore as many as you can. He has several books out there, the most popular being "2 Second Lean". The book is very insightful, inspiring and not only easy to read, but very easy to apply; 2 seconds at a time. It focuses on incremental, continuous improvement, starting small and building upon it. Paul speaks to many Lean concepts and has several references to Toyota and Japanese culture and industry.

If you go to https://paulakers.net you will find an incredible amount of Lean resources and in particular a video section containing videos showing lots of great non-manufacturing applications of Lean. The library includes examples in Farming, Governments, Health, Homes, Kids, Office, Organizations and Travel. I have found myself lost for hours on Paul's page and loved every minute of it. I must admit, I am a little jealous of how far he has taken this and the impact he is having goes way beyond his FastCap business. This is part of my aspirations, to get to his level of impact on the world. I guess I have a gap to close and would love to be having a positive impact on folks at the level he is.

These are some examples of Lean beyond manufacturing that are fairly well known and have broad impacts. The rest of the book will dive into the different, non-manufacturing ways I am applying Lean and making things better.

Don't You Want All This Value?

Value; think about that word. What does it mean to you? Is it something you desire? I tend to desire value in absolutely everything. It is interesting how widely variable people's opinions of value are. Let's start with some of the ways Merriam-Webster defines value. **Value (noun)** – 1) the monetary worth of something 2) a fair return or equivalent in goods, services or money for something exchanged 3) relative worth, utility, or importance 4) something (such as a principle or quality) intrinsically valuable or desirable 5) a numerical quantity that is assigned or is determined by calculation or measurement. **Value (verb)** – 1) to consider or rate highly 2) to estimate or assign the monetary worth of, to rate of scale in usefulness, importance, or general worth.

Well, that was clear as mud and leaves lots of room for variability, interpretation, and individualism. I am encouraged to report it does have variability and allows for individualism. The areas where I have seen sustained success with a Lean culture shift is where folks are able to define what is value to them and ultimately to the external or internal downstream customer. Once value is defined there are so many different

Lean tools and principles capable of helping you pursue that 'Value'.

I want to start with a key value for me, which is being seen as a leader. At my core I really do want people to be able to look to me with confidence to lead and I thrive on helping others achieve success. That is a key Value for me and Lean has had a major impact on my ability to realize some of the value. I measure the value by quantifying the opportunities I provide for folks to engage in that leadership dynamic and track how many people are actively seeking my leadership on that front.

I want to get into some more tangible examples of value across many types of business sectors and even a sports team. First, we will start with Toyota and value in production volume. At the beginning of Toyota's Lean Journey, Ford, GM and Chrysler accounted for 95% of all automobile sales in the United States. By 1988 the share dropped to under 30%, with cars coming from Japan filling the largest gap. The Japanese market share on the World Market also, went from near zero in 1955 to near 28% in 1988. The next interesting Toyota data point is the copycat factor. The percentage of Japanese Transplant production in the United States was near zero in 1982 and rose to over 20% by 1990. If you ask Toyota what a key value point is for Lean, they will tell you they are tapping into the knowledge and insights of their team members and capitalizing on the creativity of the employees.

Next, I would like to share some thoughts on Pixar. Pixar is a Lean company that has seen a lot of value from their culture shift. Pixar began in the late 1970's as a part of Lucasfilm's computer division and is now part of the Disney family. They produce popular animated films such as, Toy Story, Monsters, Inc., Finding Nemo, The Incredibles, Cars and many others. Their leadership over the years has also had some notable contributors including Steve Jobs, who according to their current leader Ed Catmull, is "a beacon for servant leadership that truly cares about the people." The book "Creativity Inc.", by Ed Catmull, is a great read and a must for any leader wanting to see what good looks like as it pertains to positive culture starting at the top.

Some of the Value metrics for Pixar are very impressive. First, the amount of money Disney paid to acquire this amazing Lean Company, $7.4 Billion dollars. A pretty impressive value metric if you are focused on dollars. A key thing you find out in Catmull's book is even with all of the money on the table he was very concerned about the culture and his people and wasn't as willing to deal with Disney's prior leadership as he didn't see their values aligned with his. Another impactful metric to show the success of Pixar is their streak of 14 consecutive box office #1 openings. Finally, on Pixar the list of Worldwide Box office returns is stunning, the current top three, all of which carry a $200 Million Dollar production budget are, Incredibles 2, $1.2 Billion; Toy Story 4, $1.07 Billion; and Toy Story 3, $1.06 Billion. Now add the post box office and merchandise revenue and the numbers are shocking. Good luck finding a kid that doesn't have a Pixar character-based toy, shirt or other product.

Now I want to share some value thoughts for Virgina Mason. Virginia Mason is a multiplier, they are very passionate about helping others see the value that they have found. I referenced books about Virginia Mason and those all have lots of nuggets about impact, so I will just highlight a couple here.

Let me start by giving you a little background on Virginia Mason. First, it is not in Virginia, it is in Washington State. Virginia Mason has primary care physicians, an acute care hospital, several regional medical centers, a research institute, The Virginia Mason Foundation for philanthropic efforts and to my earlier point on sharing, the Virginia Mason Institute, providing education and training on their production system for continuous improvement. Their value focus is on patient satisfaction, and the welcomed side effects have been substantial cost savings.

One example is patients calling with questions or for help have their calls answered in 3 rings or less; 20 seconds. They also get their problems answered in one call. They do not get shifted around to multiple departments or people to get answers. The folks in the call center are prepared, empowered and equipped to get people answers.

Another value they hold that proves their commitment and respect for their people is their flow and 5s processes. Which have made major strides in keeping patients on schedule, allowing employees to take their full lunch break and go home on time. I know lots of professionals in the health care industry who would faint, if that were their life; that sounds like a dream to them. They have also found value in their surgery centers with error reduction, prep time reduction, and reduced inventories resulting in more surgeries per shift. During the Lean Journey they have also helped others find value by cutting their annual harm rate in half, surpassing their targets for patient experience ratings, and reducing employee injuries. Value all over the place at Virginia Mason and very inspiring to their peers.

Another group finding value in Lean Continuous Improvement is the New Zealand All Blacks, Professional Rugby Team. It is easy to see value in professional sports. Value revolves around wins and championships. The All Blacks enjoy winning at a very high level. Their lifetime winning percentage is 77.4%, which spans 580 tests. To give some perspective, the New York Yankees lead professional baseball all time with a winning percentage of 57% and the Green Bay Packers have a slight lead over the Dallas Cowboys at 57.3% in the National Football League.

Some of the All Blacks' other Value metrics are equally impressive and prove the culture is succeeding. They are the first rugby team to win 500 international tests. They have won 10 of 16 Tri-Nation trophies, 7 of 9 World Rugby Championships, 4 of 9 Grand Slams, and held the Bledsoe cup for 19 years (2003-2021). They have also won 3 World Cups since 1987 and since the World Rankings started in 2003 they have held the #1 spot for 80% of the time. All of this coming from a country with a population of 4.9 million. To put this in perspective here are the populations of other top contenders; South Africa 57.7 million; France 65.5 million; England 55.3 million; Australia 20 million and Argentina 46 million. Very impressive not just on wins and championships, but sustainability of success. All attributed to their strong culture of continuous improvement.

Another value point, very key in our current times of battling though the COVID pandemic is the work being done at Integris. Integris is a health care system widely seen in the Lean community as somebody doing it right. Integris is a non-profit provider operating 16 hospitals across Oklahoma. They also have a full package of other care such as, rehabilitation centers, Physician Clinics, Independent Living Facilities and Pharmacies.

You will see them crediting their Lean Continuous Improvement culture as key to their response to the COVID outbreak. Their evergreen clinical guides are a great one stop shop for frontline workers trying to respond to unprecedented issues, during unprecedented times. The entire network engages in tiered huddle meetings which allow critical issues to bubble up from to the front lines to highest levels in the organization very rapidly and efficiently, not wasting time, or adding burden to already overburdened front line workers. Their use of standard work provides consistency, predictability and flexibility to shift resources as needed. Integris was very pleased with their response to COVID and gives the credit to their culture, a culture of continuous improvement.

When I talk about value and provide examples I would be remised if I didn't mention Goodyear. I currently live on the outskirts of Akron, Ohio where Goodyear has it's world headquarters. I have been incredibly privileged to learn from and pick the brain of Norbert Majerus, who retired from Goodyear and Authored a book called, "Lean- Driven Innovation." The book is jam packed with amazing examples of Lean tools and principles and how they were applied and brought value to Goodyear and not only in the tire manufacturing as one would by think, but in the Research and Development side of the business.

Goodyear is a global company not only makes tires but operating service centers with over 69,000 employees worldwide. Some of the key value metrics you will find if you dive into the Goodyear journey is cutting lead time on developing new products by 70%. In an industry where being first with a new product is a massive advantage that is key number and really drove other key Goodyear business metrics. They also made strides and brought value in the on-time deliveries which moved from 30% before Lean to 98% with a shift to a Lean Continuous Improvement Culture. Lastly, their culture shift provided value on the warranty front, where they can cite huge reductions in warranty work costs. Lean really helps get things right the first time. Lots of value in that.

Now onto my world, the Energy sector. If you ask me personally I am always going to speak to the positive impact on morale, collaboration, engagement, and happiness; you know the people stuff, the culture. The value there has been and is still being realized each day. It is corporate America, so most people will talk about different value; dollars, cycle time reductions, safety and those tangible business numbers. There is value being realized in those areas each day. I like to quantify value by the number of people in the organization seeking out improvement opportunities and collaborate to improve them. Those numbers are constantly on the rise. The interesting thing is the behavior of seeking out improvement opportunities and collaborating to improve them, results in increased value in all of the usual business categories I have mentioned above. There have been many projects focused on reducing cycle time in all parts of the business, not only on executing our capital growth and maintenance work, but on how long it takes to renew software licenses and process invoices, or order materials.

There have also been and continue to be a large number of projects that focus on reducing or eliminating waste on the cost front. The goal being to reduce our costs and save us money. Just the improvement projects I have been part of have resulted in value to the company in excess of $100 million and there are plenty of projects out there I don't get involved in at all.

Another key value point and one that really matters to a large publicly traded company like ours is accuracy and predictability in our spend and revenues. Process Mapping, Standard work, Voice of the Customer exercises, visual management, Key Behavioral Indicators (KBI) and Key Performance Indicators (KPI) as well as other lean tools and principles have generated incredible value and drastically improved our ability to be accurate and predictable.

As I wind down this Chapter on value I have to include Barry Weighmiller. Mostly because CEO Bob Chapman is an amazing example of what good looks like. You don't have to search far to find articles, quotes or clips of Mr. Chapman being an amazing, people focused Lean leader. Barry Weighmiller is a St. Louis based manufacturer with over 11,000 employees and over $24 Billion dollars in revenue. Mr.

Chapman measures value and success in the way they touch people's lives.

You can learn more about Bob Chapman in his book, "Everybody Matters, The Extraordinary Power of Caring for Your People Like Family." What a great Segway into my journey and the rest of this book, as that is what I strive to do every single day and not just the lives in my current sphere of influence, but an expanding sphere I hope has no limits.

THE PRE-JOURNEY

My Lean Journey started long before I ever knew I was on one. That may sound a bit odd, but as I started to learn Lean so many of the principles and tools seemed very familiar to me. The terminology wasn't there, but the substance was. As folks get introduced to Lean it can be amazing how much of it they are already doing. I do believe it was easy for me and others to get off the ground running with Lean if they were doing a good bit of it before they even knew what it was. To help you understand what some of those things might be and where to find them I will take some time to explain the things that jumped out to me as, 'hey I do that already' moments.

I am going to approach this from a chronological, in my life angle. The Lean things I was unknowingly doing very early were around metrics and visual management. Going back as far as middle school I was always trying to find metrics and creating visual management as it related to sports and fitness. I did Lean things like tracking critical stats in backyard wiffle-ball or football and used those stats to identify areas I needed to improve in and work on. A lot of the same logic applied to weight training and conditioning. I had an obstacle course through the woods I built and would adjust things to help close certain gaps and always timed myself and tried to beat those times. I also kept numbers on anything I was doing in the weight room and trying to adjust on the biggest gaps and areas I thought would help me get where I was heading. As an example, when basketball moved to the forefront for me I became incredibly focused on jumping higher to dunk a basketball, so leg strength and vertical jump training dominated what I was writing down, measuring and setting targets for.

It was around this same time in my life I can recall some powerful visual management showing up around the house as it related to my chores and other tasks I could be doing to earn money. There was a diagram hanging on the fridge that got checked off and the check marks got converted into dollar amounts. Not to brag, but my 3 sisters never even got close to collecting as many check marks and thus money as I did.

As I reflect on that time in my life, I also became very process oriented. Some of the ways I was earning money was based on how much I got done, not how many hours it took. I really wanted to be out earning money, but I had a much stronger desire to be competing with friends in whatever we were getting after that day, so getting things done efficiently, without defect, became critical and incredibly valuable to me. The way I delivered on my newspaper route was constantly being adjusted to get it done faster. That included how I set the papers up to be delivered, the order I delivered, the time of day, anything and everything was on the table to develop a process to get it done better and faster. The logic and approach was applied to mowing lawns and washing the town's mail truck. I refined the tools, steps and overall process as much as I could to get those tasks done and earn money;

constantly reducing the cycle time and bringing the value I was seeking.

The same drives and desires were still alive and well while I was in college. However, I don't recall me identifying many opportunities during that time, so I don't have any good examples to share. Lean behaviors did return in my first career job after college. I was staring a career as a Professional Land Surveyor and the bulk of our work was in Land Title Work, which required me to visit sites all over the area we served, covering 14 states. On those sites I collected measurements later shown on drawings companies would use to assist in acquisitions. These were retail stores, gas station, and fast food establishments among others. They were all a little different, but the process was the same and speed was key. I would get a very long list on a Monday morning and have an expectation to get it done, so I had to constantly be seeking ways to achieve my goal. I began to put more time into planning logistics. I flew about 40 times on the corporate plane and drove over 100,000 miles the first year, so logistics were incredibly important.

I also took notes on what I would do once I got to the site and kept tweaking those steps to improve efficiency. That same mentality found its way into the office side of the job as well. As I reflect back, a Lean without knowing it approach was even more important in the office as there were far more people involved in the process there. It was key to develop steps, checklist and communication tools that maximized the efficiency of the entire team. It was not helpful to anyone to have someone waiting to do their part, so the better everything could flow the better the results and experience was for everyone.

The last nugget I will share from this time in my career is around equipment storage and accessibility. We used a lot of different equipment and at different points in the process, so having it easily accessible when you needed it was key. Perhaps even more important, and you can guess how I learned this, the equipment needs to be there when you need it. If you get to the garage at 4:00 a.m. and drive 8 hours to start your work and realize you don't have what you need, you are not going to be very efficient. It turns out I was doing 5s before I ever heard of it or saw it and it was incredibly valuable to me, and the company I was working for.

As I moved to the next phase in my professional journey the opportunities for me to be Lean without even knowing came in bunches. I took a position as an Assistant Project Manager in a firm providing several types of engineering in many business sectors across several states. I even got to dabble in some international work.

I can tell you this, they display a Lean culture at a very high level and don't even know they are doing it, they just know they are seeing professional and financial success. I still keep in touch with folks there even though I have moved on and they are still knocking it out of the park. That company was much larger than the first one I worked at and handled a very diverse package of work, so metrics, visual management and process were even more critical to keep that big machine moving.

I am going to date myself a little here and if you are in the next generations this will sound crazy to you, but in the early 2000's they had key metrics and information streaming on flat screens all over the place. I felt like I was in an episode of the Jetsons the first time I saw it. It was not just the way they visually managed the metrics, but the metrics they were tracking and sharing. The metrics were consistent across different areas, very intuitive and most importantly drove desired behavior to achieve desired results. I was wrapped up in the middle of all of this and progressing forward at a great pace. I was being Lean and didn't even know it, neither did they, but it worked.

As I think back to some of the specific metrics in place at the time they were actually using a Key Behavior Indicator (KBI). Not only did I not know that as Lean back then, I didn't really wrap my head around the concept until well into my Lean journey. The KBI concept is now something I think about every single day. The KBI fixes problems before they become a result. I have had arguments about calling these leading indicators and they are, but I make certain to call them Key Behavior Indicators. I think it is extremely important to make sure the people in a process are fully aware of what the process is and their behaviors within that process produce the results. I said it before and I will say it again, desired behaviors produce desired results.

Another place they used solid metrics was in business development. It came to a point where leadership knew they had to diversify and expand their business. They were incredibly successful with the current pool of clients and had and very high repeat business rate, but a major economic bubble was about to burst in this country and there was a lot of concern about where that would leave the current client pool. The leadership had a great understanding of the fact it takes many leads to generate an actual opportunity and several opportunities to generate a successful contract. Therefore, they set goals and provided visual management around those data points. The teams really got energized and put some focus on seeking new business; the desired behavior, bringing great value.

Another behavior happening there I would consider Lean without knowing it is their investment in technology. I feel their focus on leveraging technology displays Respect for People. They are not shy about going out and getting the best technology to help employees complete their work faster and easier. This includes vehicles, field equipment, office equipment, software and even the office spaces they work in. All state of the art and geared towards making work easier and faster for the people out there getting it done.

When I think back to the vehicles, they were on a whole other level than anything I had previously seen. The trucks were set up with secured caps, multiple alternators and batteries, printers, storage boxes and workspaces allowing charging and storage of equipment as well as doing some office work in the field, all designed to make things easier and more efficient. You no longer have to drag everything into the office and put it on a charger every night, or risk showing up on a site to work, while your battery is on the charger at the office. Everything had a place and every place made sense for the flow of the work. It was very impressive. It was also very Lean and we didn't even know it.

With all of the technology and all the cool stuff, overhead can become a hinderance in a very competitive market. The counterbalance to increased overhead is sound and efficient process. If you are going to have all the cool toys, you have to get it done faster to be competitive. We had processes for everything and we were always seeking ways to improve those processes. That goes top to bottom, in the field, in the office and even in the marketing and business development space. The processes and tools developed to help Project Managers find and capitalize on new opportunities were very slick and incredibly efficient, again dating myself, but at the time GIS (Geographic Information Systems) was new and not a lot of companies were using it for anything, especially something like business development, but we were and it was a huge advantage.

As I look back on those days with the Lean knowledge I have now, there were Lean things thriving in that culture that I still haven't been able to get off the ground in my current role, and still aspire to achieve. I guess that is why it is a journey and may not always be heading in the same direction. There will be setbacks.

What I consider my pre-journey had one more stop before I got my powerful introduction to the formal Lean Six Sigma business mentality. It was another engineering firm supplying multiple engineering services to several different business sectors, and at the time a bigger client base in the energy sector, which was the main driver behind my move. I was very fortunate my old team wanted to come over and work with me again and I was in a leadership position where I had lots of autonomy to lead the team as I saw fit. We were very Lean and didn't even know it.

Lots of our energy contracts and even some of our retail development contracts were paid on units, so we got paid x amount of dollars for x amount of work. The visibility of the metrics and documented processes, which were always being updated, had a big impact on those metrics. They were key to not only our financial success, but our engagement, collaboration, team strength, and our happiness. It was really fun to chase success as a team with great alignment and full engagement.

The cycle time reductions made by documenting Standard Operating Procedures (SOP's) and updating them every time we found a better way were massive and gave us an incredible advantage. Providing engineering consulting services in the energy sector is not only extremely competitive; lots of lions fighting for the same steak, but it required accurate work free of defects. You had to do it fast and it had to be right, no excuses. This is another arena where the SOP's really helped. They included several visual tools and lots of checklists that really helped ensure things were complete and accurate. If all the boxes are checked you have a great shot at no defects. The standardization, checklists and visual tools started all the way back to where a new project was bid and were carried all the way through the final deliverable to the client and the lesson learned and data storage on our end.

As I begin to wind down this chapter, I not only hope one of these Lean-without-knowing-it examples can help you, but I hope you can look back at things that have gone well in your life or business and consider if it would fit into a Lean culture. My guess is it would. I do firmly believe these experiences and my ability to connect them to what a Lean culture is made it very easy for me to get started and have faith it is the right thing to do. I don't remember a time when I asked, does this stuff actually work, mostly because I already had many examples of Lean working.

I am actively involved in shifting the culture in my current career stop. I have seen success in showing teams that some of the valuable things they are currently doing is actually Lean. All of that is why I felt it is very important to have this chapter in the book and hope it helps you on your journey. I also hope this chapter provides a key to unlock the door blocking somebody you are trying to get moving on their own journey.

THE JOURNEY STARTS

My first day on the industry side of the energy sector I got thrown directly into Lean and began a more formal Lean journey, Japanese terms included. I walked into a conference room and there were several rolls of paper in a pile. I was told you are the process owner for these 5 process workflows. It was the first time I have ever seen a process workflow and I was a bit overwhelmed, but instantly saw some value in the content and format sitting in front of me. The pessimistic excitement must have been very visible to the folks around me because I was quickly told "don't worry you will be getting an introduction to Lean training very shortly". As it turned out, my first day was near the tail end of the first month the teams in the area I was working in were starting their Lean journey. It was a foreign language for everyone, not just me.

As the prior chapter states, once the trainings began in earnest it clicked very easy for me and the excitement began to build without hesitation. The first training was a small in-house built suite of introductory trainings lasting about a day and half, touching on Servant Leadership, Respect for People,

Voice of the Customer, Visual Management and Gemba Walks. Of those, even though 90% of the examples in the training were Toyota, I was able to connect easily to all of them with my past experiences, except Gemba Walks.

What I know now is I was doing them without knowing it. In the training however there was a big stress on the fact that if you are in a leadership role, which I was at the time, you are not there to dispense solutions. You don't go out there to fix their problems. You go out there to empower, inspire and motivate the front-line team members to fix their own problems by helping remove the hurdles they identify. You will need to put your ego aside and not dispense solutions. I immediately stepped back from this idea like it was a coiled-up cobra ready to strike. I felt like I knew me, and I was a solution guy. I love solving problems, especially problems others are struggling with. How in the world was I going to not dispense solutions? I completely understood the importance of my behavior as a leader and completely believed in the philosophy behind it but didn't think I possessed the skill to do it well. I took the training again over a year later and was a shadow on a couple of Gemba Walks done by leaders who possess that skill. I now feel extremely comfortable, not only doing a Gemba Walk, but helping and coaching other leaders wanting to do Gemba Walks.

My progress on the Gemba Walk front is a very strong example of this being a journey. I didn't think I would get as far as I am, considering where I started. Otherwise, the things I was learning as Lean all clicked, all made sense and I was ready to go.

The next key phase in the journey was within the first 90 days I was sent to Oklahoma for a formal Lean Six Sigma White Belt Training put on by the University of Oklahoma. I still have the certification in the nice frame they provided it in. A little side note, I am a huge Oklahoma Sooners fan and have been since I was a young kid. It has been Boomer Sooner in my world for a long, long time, so seeing that big O-U on a formal piece of paper with my name on it is pretty cool. The interesting thing about White Belt Training; which is an 8-hour class introducing Lean Six Sigma at a fairly high level. I didn't learn a whole lot of new stuff, mostly some buzz words; but it reaffirmed what I was seeing work.

In my first 90 days we were actively engaged in Lean. We were utilizing our past experiences as well as the day and a half training. The 8-hour class was essentially a confirmation of; you guys know what you are doing. I have to make sure I am crystal clear on this because I know my journey, and also the journey of dozens of my peers and not all Lean Journeys escalate as quickly as mine did. This can take time to evolve. I had amazing trust, tons of respect and lots of support coming from my direct leadership, the General Manager of our area at the time. I also had a team of 7 I was empowering the best I could, and they were engaged, bought in, excited and happy to be on the journey. I also think it is key to note some of the early improvements we took on had some short cycle times, we knew in 1-2 months on several improvements if they actually worked or not. That is not typical in our environment, some of the front-end process improvements will take 2-3 years to have definitive data to prove it worked, so we got a little lucky there.

It was becoming very clear the leadership support, our quick results and my passion for the topic was a bit contagious as I was being asked to help other teams and leaders get going on a Lean journey. It was at this point a manager in another department, much larger than mine, was moving into a different role and they approached me about combining that team with my existing team. I had no formal training or really sound background in what that department did, but they were not looking for me to provide technical or operational knowledge. The focus was completely on helping them shift towards a Lean culture and start reducing and eliminating waste all while expanding their understanding of the full value stream.

Our world is extremely fast paced, very complex and a bit cutthroat, so a lot of teams tend to dig in and get laser focused on hitting their dates and their budgets and it can be difficult to see beyond that. A lot of times you may be saving a dollar and costing someone else ten. The same approach I had leveraged previously proved helpful in this environment and major strides were made on the cost, predictability, schedule and full value stream front. I once again found myself fortunate to be empowered, trusted and supported from not only leadership, but the teams I was fortunate to lead.

It was during this time we were going through a pretty substantial merger and there were not only lots of moving parts and adjustments being made to roles and processes, but lots of people were let go from the company. It was an extremely difficult time for me. As I mentioned earlier Respect for People is paramount to me and this type of activity doesn't sit well. I certainly didn't agree with a lot of what was going on around me at this time, but knew if I was patient, persistent and focused on that which I can influence and control I can have a positive impact in an otherwise negative time. I would be lying if I said it was easy, it certainly was not.

My journey, my career and my livelihood were all in jeopardy at this point. I went back and forth thinking, "is this worth it?" I mentioned earlier, this hasn't always been a forward moving journey for me, it had some shifts backward. I did learn a lot at this time and in particular about myself. I began leveraging standard work, visual management and KPI's around my mental wellbeing and habits. I had metrics and visual management on things like persistence and patience and started making some very visual roadmaps on where I wanted to go personally, professionally, and physically. All things I still have in place today.

Once again, my results, persistence and passion was a bit contagious and despite a major leadership shift in my world, which seemed to be the new normal; 11 bosses in 8 years; I was being tasked by leaders outside of my silo to get involved and help out in other organizations. I call it a silo on purpose, our business units are very segmented and we all know it is a problem and we are on a journey to make it better. It was nice to get exposure, respect and trust from a whole new group of people, especially because they are a key downstream customer of the processes the group I was working in executes. This gave me so much more perspective as I spent my whole career in the upfront, designing portion and these teams were downstream operating what was already designed and built.

Training and exposure to Lean really began to take off here and there were tons of in-house Lean classes being offered, all of which I took, some more than once. There was also some on-line courses out there, all of which I took. Within these trainings there were a lot of book recommendations.

As far as me being a reader that is also a pretty interesting journey. In high school and college I avoided reading at all costs. I absolutely hated it. When I first got out of college I was flying a lot and being almost 6'6" tall and all legs. I was insanely uncomfortable on a plane, sleeping was not an option. It was here I began to read as a distraction, no non-fiction, mostly biographies and historical books. I got sucked in big time and began reading more often, eventually 5 or more days a week. The bulk was historical topics, lots of World War II and Civil War books, and biographies of people I look up to. People like, Muhammad Ali, Jack Dempsey, Abraham Lincoln, Shaquille O'Neal and anything New England Patriots. Tedy Bruschi's book, "Never Give Up" talks about his return to professional football after suffering a stroke. It is very inspiring. I actually started reading a lot, and not just on planes, so when key Lean books were being recommended I was jumping all over it. I now have shelves and shelves of not only historical non-fiction books, but also personal growth, continuous improvement and Lean focused books.

A little side note here, as I read I typically keep a high-lighter handy and highlight key take aways. That makes it very easy to go back and refresh myself or share with others key items from the amazing library I have developed. That little nugget is also why I may never switch to e-books or anything like that, I can't lose that value. Some of those key books are mentioned throughout this book and all of them are on the book list at the end. I also turned this into a fun and exciting adventure on YouTube. I started doing, "Behind the High-lighter" interviews with authors. I ask them questions about what I highlighted in their books. It has been so much fun and I plan to expand that effort as far as willing authors will let me.

I also began to gain a new, profound understanding of how important perspective is. I created an entry fee for my office. I hung a sign on the door letting everyone know if you walked into my office you were required to take a book from my bookshelf, turn to a page that has something highlighted, read it and talk to me about it. What an amazing program, very impactful for me to gain lots of different perspective, but also impactful for the person interacting with me. Many times, they asked to borrow the book and read the rest, but every time, I witnessed them go into deep thought and open up. Often times about things that are difficult to talk about, like disrespect for people and poor behavior by leadership. I actu-ally had several folks would walk in just to learn and talk.

I recall one time a Vice President in the Company walked in and said, "Do I actually have to do this"? I said "You do. It was clearly posted on the door it is required". Nothing jumped off the shelf to him, so I grabbed Tim Eisenhauer's book,

"Who The Hell Wants to Work For You". As the title indicated this book is full of examples of bad leadership behavior, as well as better options. This particular VP in our company turned to a page that was pretty blunt, as most of the book is. It was something being spoken about as being a terrible behavior that leaders typically display and I feel was on display every day in our company, so I was on the edge of my chair and eager to see if his ego was going to make an excuse or disagree. It didn't go that way.

I asked if he thinks that happens here and without hesitation he said, "Yes!" So, I asked, is that aright and again without hesitation he said, "No!". So, what are you going to do about it? The answer was "I am not sure. It would be very difficult to change". That is not the exact answer I was hoping for, but in our culture at the time, someone in a Senior Leadership role admitting we were wrong was huge and a great first step. This program was so amazing and if you have the books, personality and environment to do something similar I would encourage you do so. For me, COVID moved us to work from home and now the only thing coming into my office is one of my dogs, so I lost this and miss it dearly. I am contemplating trying to get a virtual version going if you call me for something. I get calls all day.

The success I am having and this absolute thirst for Lean learning really pulled me into the next key step in my journey. Which was a formal, Lean Six Sigma Green Belt Certification. This program for us was 10 full days of classroom work, a presentation to the class, an exam which you had to pass and then completion of a project you had to be coached not only through the problem and project identification, but through the completion of the project. The class was amazing and I couldn't get enough of it. Not only was the instructor someone familiar to me that I hold in a very high regard, but my classmates were amazing. There was a ton of diversity in background, experience and roles within the company. The room was full of positive energy, collaboration and excitement all 10 days. Such a great learning environment. I took the exam very seriously and really buckled down and prepared with near perfect results, another indicator I am getting this stuff.

The next step was finding and completing a project. This proved to be fairly difficult and took months. At the time I would guess less than 10% of our 4,000+ employees understood Lean and were doing anything with it. That meant finding an opportunity that has a sound process and data clearly showing a performance gap was really difficult. In retrospect it ended up being a blessing. I think I filled in 12 different 8-step problem solving models, up to the 3rd box; which is 'set improvement targets'. This proved to be great practice and really helped me learn. I started them in a word document since that is the template we were given but pivoted quickly to doing them on a white board. That is what I still do today.

We just didn't have processes and KPI's producing usable data for a problem statement. I really learned a lot about how important process development, discipline and measurement is. Those were all lessons I carry forward today and leverage constantly.

Finally, a project came up that can help me achieve this formal next step in my journey. The opportunity did not have readily available gap data, but the folks in the process knew it was worth going and getting the data. We sprang into action developing the measurement needed to take all the grey out of the perceived problem and get to the facts. It took some time to get the measurement systems in place and gather enough data to clearly define the problem.

Once we did, it was clearly a pretty big opportunity, millions of dollars a year, just in the small area we were looking at. The number can be multiplied across the country as other areas were likely either having or going to have the same problem. I served in the facilitator role on the improvement project team and was very fortunate to have a strong sponsor and team lead. If you can get that on your own journey for formal improvement projects please do. It is imperative. As everything came together the best Lean tool for the team and this problem was a Rapid Improvement Event (RIE), which I facilitated. It turned out to be very successful, earning me my Lean Six Sigma Green Belt Certification. A little side note here, lots of folks hear Rapid Improvement Event and think it is fast. That is not all together true. The actual event is, however the pre-work of defining the problem, identifying the team and getting everything organized and ready can be far from rapid.

Now that I have another piece of paper displaying some credibility for me what is next? The logical next step for most in the Black Belt Certification. I decided I wanted to keep applying what I already have learned and take some time before I start the next leg of my journey. What I found is in my current environment there is little value for me to pursue that next step. We don't have a ton of well defined processes that are being followed and producing piles of data needing that level of expertise. As my experience here uncovered those conditions I had to adjust where my focus was going to be. I want to have the highest impact. My focus had to shift to the culture and more specifically respect, engagement and empowerment of the teams getting the work done at the front lines.

There were some really key things happening at this time and my mind was racing so fast that the advice I got the most was, slow down, pump the brakes, not everyone has your passion for this. At the time hearing that was deflating and made me think I needed out and should be looking to go somewhere that my passion would be appreciated. I am glad I got over that hump, as this became a valuable learning experience for me. I learned your passion for something should be a benefit, not a detriment and if you can learn how to leverage that passion to motivate, inspire and get people interested all while meeting them where they are, you can have a major impact and provide a lot of help, support and value to lots of folks. You can't help the ones you scare off, so don't scare them off.

As I struggled through some frustrations, I was throwing a lot of things at the wall to see what would stick and my stick rate was very low. Proof again that this is not always a forward moving journey. There will be setbacks. I couldn't help but ask myself, "why am I here struggling to find the magic wand or silver bullet to get the culture to shift, when thousands of folks have already figured that out and some of them are sharing it"? I began to research and learn from others on how they got it to go. There were dozens of great finds on this part of my journey and the pace of my progress increased substantially. The next chapter is going to provide more detail on who some of the folks are and how much it is impacting my journey. Don't miss out on learning about those great people and resources.

THE IMPACT OF OTHERS ESCALATES THE PACE OF THE JOURNEY

As you could imagine the process of writing this book has been an amazing exercise for me on reflection. And not just reflection on how far I have come, but on what really helped. As I write and try to share the things that brought value and helped with my journey, I am also thinking about what those things are that were absolutely required? What are those things that if they were not present, there would be no Journey, no value, no stories to share, no ideas to share.

That leads me to the thought that the single biggest thing I needed was a network of people. It would have been catastrophic had I not been fortunate to have a network of great people around me. I needed, and still need people to teach, inspire and motivate me. I need people to provide a different perspective. I need people to gratify me, to let me know what I am doing is bringing value and I need people to just listen and let me vent. I am going to spend some time here talking about some of those people and why they were critical path on my journey. There are far too many people to speak about or even list here, so I am just going to highlight some key and unique ones.

The prior chapter touched on some of these people and impacts. I am going to get into more detail here about these folks and the key impacts they had and continue to have. I want to be clear that most of the people fall into more than one category, so I am just going to speak to where they have the biggest and most unique impacts for me. I am going to put them into several important categories. I believe it will help you greatly to have folks in these roles on your journey. It is easy for me to know who to talk about and to explain why they are important. The hardest part of this chapter is to know what to call them, so here is my best shot. The impactful roles are, the 'Starter', 'Embracer', 'Truster', 'Multiplier', 'Sound Board', 'Adjuster', 'Outsider', 'Persister', and 'Supporter'. As I am structuring this Chapter I realize that I am one of these for a lot of folks, so not only do you need people in these roles, you need to be these things for others.

First, the 'Starter'. Simply enough the person who had the biggest single impact of inspiring you to start your Lean Journey. I do think this needs to be more than just the first person that used the term Lean. Just hearing the term is not nearly enough to inspire someone to start a Journey like this. It needs to be more inspiring and more motivating than that. For me the 'Starter' is Brian deFonteny. Brian was one of the instructors in the early Lean classes I took. He has become far, far more than that to me. I would say he fired the starting gun for a very long race I was about to run. Not only did he really get me started through inspiration and motivation, but he has and is part of the rest of the journey. He continues to be a friend, inspiration and major part of my support system even in his retirement. I often try to block out an hour or so to chat with Brian and find myself on the phone for hours and needing to plug the phone in to continue the conversation because the battery failed to keep up with our Lean chat. There have been a lot of key moments with Brian, and I could talk for days about him and his impact, but I want to focus on something that I feel was a unique impact on my journey. That is the start.

Brian provided an "ah-ha" moment for me that I remember today as if it happened this morning. It is something he said in a very engaging and inspiring training that he was leading. If you ever sat through one of his trainings, you can't possibly leave without noticing the passion he has for the topic. It is on display and unavoidable. He said very plainly and with a ton of energy, "I absolutely love coming to work every day and love what I do". I instantly thought, I want that, now how do I get it? I enjoyed my job and most of the time enjoyed coming to work but was I standing on a mountain top shouting out that I love what I do, and I love coming to work, as he was? I was not. So, am I on that mountain top shouting now? The answer is............, more often than I used to, but not all the time. I still have room for improvement. I am trending in the right direction. If you want more of Brian's insight; 'Leadership Reimagined', by Brian deFonteny is out there and a great book. I have not only read it several times and turn back to sections I highlighted as key points from time to time, but I have given it as a gift to several friends and family members. Finally, where I want to leave you with Brian is that there is no doubt he was the 'Starter'. His inspiration and motivation was extremely impactful. If you already found your starter great, make sure they know it. If you haven't; go seek one, there are plenty of them out there. Maybe it's me?

Now onto the 'Embracer'. That is a person who is already embracing Lean. They don't need some elaborate sales pitch, they are on board. They also embrace and support your energy and passion for Lean. The 'Embracer' should preferably be in some sort of formal leadership role. That will make things a lot easier. For me, I got a little lucky here, it was my direct Manager at the time, Kris. Kris was not only a believer in Lean, but had an understanding and appreciation of the Respect for People piece. He was all about empowering others and building a team. He also appreciated and encourage my passion and abilities on the Lean front. This was helpful as my journey was very young and I was definitely learning a lot and certainly not an expert.

I found myself needing his formal authority to help remove some of those early hurdles. I am not sure the journey would have made it very far without the early embracing, support and flexibility to fail. There is a lot I appreciate about Kris and the role he played in my journey.

One of the key things that I think helped him embrace what I was about to embark on and really contributed to the relationship developing was his focus on metrics that mattered. Several of those metrics were very business focused like; cost savings, quality assurance and reduced cycle time, but he also was interested in people metrics. He was famous for placing valuable metrics were people had to notice them, like bathroom stalls and the common kitchen area. He had a strong interest in people collaborating. I can recall him speaking about the sounds he heard coming from the main conference room.

That is where most of the impactful working meetings were happening. His office was on the opposite side of the wall so he could easily hear things like full engagement, active pace, excitement, and laughter. Guess what, you can have fun and still get work done and he was proud of the team environment and fun that was very evident. His embracing of Lean showed up amongst the masses.

Next the 'Truster'. This is the person that puts some trust in you. They show a little faith that this new thing you are starting is going to be Ok. In some ways they are allowing your actions to impact some portions of their future. It is very helpful to have somebody around that trusts you. Someone that trusts that your journey is bringing value, trusts they can team up with you and gain value for them, and trust that you will not waste their time. For me that is Dwayne.

Dwayne was a key member of a great team that I was in the care of. We made some major strides on the Lean front and were producing some very impressive results. We also began helping other teams within their space. As our scope and influence expanded Dwayne took on more and more and without hesitation. Dwayne showed incredible Trust in what we where doing and the expansion of influence we were taking on. His Trust in me was highly impactful and beneficial to helping me sustain and be energized around continuing my Journey. Get some folks around you that Trust what you are doing, you will not regret it.

Now onto the 'Multipliers'. These are the folks that are actively pulling knowledge from me and seeking my advice and input. Not only seeking the knowledge but converting the knowledge into actionable items. They are taking what they are learning from you and using it to have valuable impacts without you. They are teaching and inspiring others, thus multiplying the impact you are having. The book, "Unstoppable Teams", by Alden Mills has a Chapter called, "Activating the 10X advantage". It speaks to having a full team of folks aligned to have valuable impacts. Those impacts can be much larger and occur faster if there are multiple people out there driving it.

For me, there may be no better indicator that you are doing something right, than others wanting to follow in your footsteps. I am a multiplier for Brian and I make sure he knows it. For me, there are actually several 'Multipliers' out there now. I am always seeking to grow that number and actually track it. I want to start with the first one, because without him I would not have moved forward at the pace I have. The first 'Multiplier' for me was Doug. There were some days that were a struggle and I felt like, well as long as it is making things better for him it is worth it. Doug is now aggressively on his own journey and is still a key piece in my journey. He is not shy about telling me about the impact I have had on him and the impact he is having on others. He is truly and actively taking my Lean knowledge and multiplying the impact.

There have been several occasions where Doug has magically showed up and helped me through tough times. His gratitude for what he has learned from me not just professionally, but on the self improvement and home front certainly puts a little pep in my step. The positive feedback about Doug I get from around the company really does warm my heart and gives me a sense of pride. You have to be happy about the fact that the impacts you are having are being paid forward by others. The reach and value increases much faster if you have a couple of Dougs around you as part of your Journey.

Next, the 'Sound Board'. This is the person that puts you on the psychology couch and listens, gives you a chance to vent and get things off your chest. This is a tough role for a lot of people. I currently find myself in this role for several folks. When the frustrations and doubt creep in, you need someone around that can listen. If you are doing this right you will understand that it takes time. You are changing behaviors, breaking habits and impacting culture. None of that is done overnight. You have to bring folks along at their pace and that can be incredibly frustrating. It is very hard to stand by and know how much better things can be for someone and you can't get them out of their own way, or the bosses are a major hurdle.

The boss hurdle is one that really bothers me and I still struggle with today. The Boss hurdle is also the one my Sound Board helped me with the most. Jason was and is my 'Sound

Board'. I do not call on him as often as I once did and I think
that is a great indicator that he did his job well. He really did
provide a lot of guidance and advice that I still lean on today
to get me by. He was and still is in a formal Senior Leadership
position within the company and I think that dynamic helped
me out a lot.

As I mentioned earlier we are very siloed and it is important to note he was not in my Silo. I think that was actually
beneficial. He also had a lot of experience navigating the
corporate structure and is a far more patient and understanding man than I. He has a great understanding and appreciation of Lean. I believe he also serves as a great Sound Board
for me because of his focus and passion for the Respect for
People pillar of Lean. He has always been very open and vocal
about his opinion that he thinks this is the most important
pillar and also the one we need the most work on. As your
journey progresses and you become more and more aware of
what 'Good' looks like, your frustrations for what is 'Not
Good' will grow and your 'Sound Board' will be on speed dial.

Another key member of my journey I am calling the
'Adjuster'. This is person who provides some course correc-
tion. Someone who offers a fresh approach, perspective, or
idea. As my journey hit what seemed like insurmountable
hurdles I found myself in desperate need of a new angle-of-
attack, a new approach, a fresh perspective. It was at this time I
stumbled across Paul Akers. This happened very much by acci-
dent. I heard an Akers board mentioned in a meeting I was in
and had to ask, "What the heck is that"? I am so glad I did.
Instead of a direct answer I was guided to a web site. A web
site I got lost on for hours just absorbing piles and piles of
amazing Lean knowledge. A good bit of which was coming at
Lean from a very different angle and approach then I had seen
previously. Paul takes a two second Lean approach.

The two second Lean approach tries to make small two

second improvements each day. He and his teams are an amazing resource for outside of the box thinking on continuous improvement. His book, "2-Second Lean" had an immediate impact on me and I reference it still. I began documenting and improving my morning routine the day after I finished reading it. I made small tweaks every single day and before I knew it the list of things I could cross off before my actual work day started was incredibly long. I share Paul's information constantly and love hearing from people about how much of an impact it had on them. In my world, the second biggest hurdle related to converting the culture to Lean is time. If I had a nickel for each time I heard, "I am too busy for Lean" I would not be working the hours I am and would have got this book done much sooner. Paul's approach makes this manageable for even the busiest of non-Leaners out there. He made a major adjustment to my approach and gave me another tool in the tool box to get people moving in the right direction.

I have to also mention while I am on the Paul Akers celebration train, that his book, "Lean Health" was also incredibly impactful and continues to have a major impact on me. He somehow also made being healthy very simple. Get 10,000 steps, do some push ups, do some sit ups and get most of your calories from fruit, vegetables and nuts. When I read the book I was lingering around the 280lb mark. It took me less than 30 days to get down under 250 and I have been under 245 for at least 75% of the year for the last 5 years. I measure my weigh almost every Friday and mark off if I am over or under 245. That seems to be the weight that I am the happiest at. I set a goal for myself to make sure I stay under that at least 75% of the year and have had no problem doing so, likely because of the simplicity of it.

Now onto the 'Outsider'. I call this person the outsider because the knowledge I was gaining from them never once mentions Lean. The principles and behaviors are drenched in Respect for People and Continuous Improvement but this person is not known as a Lean advocate or practitioner. It is imperative to have someone you can point to that is doing it right without all the Lean lingo to help the hardcore, "this is not for me", folks to start moving in the right direction. For me, I found that person in Simon Sinek. If you have not seen any of his TED talks or YouTube videos do yourself a favor and block some time out to do so. He is best known for his talks and books, "Start With Why" and "Leaders Eat Last". I have guided many anti-Leaners toward Simon Sinek and have seen amazing results.

I start almost all of my Lean communications with 'Why' because of Simon. I also encourage others to do the same and our current Improvement Sharing standard for the company is based on Simon's Golden Circle which is discussed in his talks and starts with; you guessed it..... 'Why'. If you can't find anyone else that is not directly associated with Lean to utilize in this capacity save yourself some time and effort and use Simon. His impact on the people here has been incredible.

Another key member of my network and substantial contributor to my Journey I am going to call my;'Persistor'. This person provided advice at a very pivotal moment about persistence. He also had a Lean Journey that had some hurdles and set backs and his advice to me to be persistent and think about how worth it this will be if you can make this happen really shaped my path. I am extremely glad he was there. The 'Persistor' for me is Norbert Majerus. Norbert is a very well know Lean advocate, Shingo Prize Winner, Author, consultant, presenter and amazing resource. In his book he lays out what he calls the inside out approach to a Lean implementation and those steps have really helped me on my journey. I found it interesting that none of the steps were really new to me. I was doing pretty much all of them. The order in which they are taken and the dependency they have on each other is the part that was new. It instantly made sense and I made a very quick pivot to follow those steps.

For some the President or CEO of the company is driving the Lean culture shift providing a top down approach. I have talked with some people in this environment and not much persistence is needed there. Things move very quickly, folks get engaged and are energized around continuous improvement almost instantaneously. That was not the case for me and still is not. The further up our org chart you go, the less energy there is around Lean. Norbert was in a similar situation and not only did the inside out approach help him on his journey, but some persistence was required. I find myself trying to leverage his inside out approach on my journey and am very much aware that so far persistence has been a major factor in my success.

As I struggled and started looking more to what others were doing I certainly found myself confronted with opportunities to take my passion and skill set elsewhere. Maybe, even somewhere that appreciated it more and would be far better at removing hurdles for me to be successful than my current role. I would call this the easy path. Where the easy path can also be the best path, I believe if I took the easy path at that point in my career I would have missed out on some extremely impactful experiences. I distinctly remember being in a presentation that Norbert was offering around Lean Project Management and everything he was saying was hitting home. He has a great appreciation and focus for the Respect for People pillar of Lean. I found myself very engaged and asking a lot of questions. I was noticing others in the room engaging and responding to some of my questions.

I couldn't help but get a feeling that there may be some job offers coming my way from the dialogue happening. I was not actively looking for a job, but my mind sure did start to wonder, what if I could find myself on the easy path? During a break he approached me to discuss some of the things that I spoke to and made a comment about the struggles I must be facing and how the culture didn't sound conducive or receptive to my approach. He was pretty spot on and I began to share my thoughts about maybe wanting to be in an environment that was more embracing and supportive of my efforts. He very quickly turned me completely around by speaking to the fact that if I have the energy and persistence to make it happen where I am it will be very worthwhile. It is about the journey and the impact you can have. I had and still have the drive, energy and passion to change behaviors and improve culture, so how well utilized would I be in a company that doesn't need that as much.

I have pinged Norbert from time to time and he always answers the call. He presents a lot all over the world and I try to catch as many as I can. He has certainly been a catalyst for me to remain persistent and keep working towards the change I desire to see on the not so easy path. Find a 'Persister', someone that encourages and inspires you to remain persistent on your journey.

Finally, I had what I will tag a 'Supporter'. I desperately needed someone in the top end of the org chart to support my efforts. I had a ton of support from the front lines, some support from middle management and even some high-level folks outside of my organization supporting my efforts, but the upper-level support within the organization I was directly supporting was missing. I was reporting directly to the Vice President of Engineering and Construction for the Northeast. He was just starting to get some formal exposure to Lean. I knew I had a chance. It was just going to take some confidence, persistence, proven results and a little luck to get him on board.

I can generate all of those except the luck, which showed

up when he became incredibly focused on getting some consistency in the four different business units that existed within the overall Northeast organization that he was responsible for. Enter me, my passion for continuous improvement and my vast experience with process mapping. I wish I could tell you it was as easy as showing him how a process map works and off we go, but it was not. It took some time, effort and lots of metrics to get the needle moving. Eventually, it did move and I found an opportunity to propose an effort that would get him all in. I was doing Lean and helping others do Lean. However, per the company roles and responsibilities for the job title I was holding, helping others do Lean was not in there anywhere.

We just went through a downsizing and reorganization of the company that left his team without any formal Lean or Continuous improvement resource. Those that never had it were in danger of never getting it and those that had it were in danger of losing it. I made a proposal to keep my day job and be given a very formal role of Value Stream Manager for his organization as a night job. It was a bit of a nerve-racking proposal being that we had just gone through a reduction in force and massive reorganization of the company and here I am saying lets shuffle the deck again, I need a new role. Fortunately, for me, and eventually for the organization we got past the initial shock of the request very quickly and were moving forward with the proposal by the next business day.

Here is Senior Leadership support that I desperately needed and in a very official and impactful way. Glenn was and still is a Senior Level 'Supporter' that has significantly benefited my Lean journey.

Lean at Work; the Obvious

Value at work can be defined in many ways and is highly dependent on what type of work you are doing and where you sit within the organization. A key value that I would hope everyone holds regardless of the type of work and your seat in the org chart is people; people being safe and people being happy. A key pillar of Lean; Respect for People, if taken seriously and being a key part of the focus; like it should be, takes care of this. I know I just made that sound very simple; it is not. It does take focus, effort and experience to do this well. I find myself learning something on this front constantly.

When you talk value at work many will also point to the more classic business numbers like profit, revenue, cycle time and customer satisfaction. Lean can support growth in the workplace in every single one of those categories. Not only can it support it, but I have seen impacts in all of those categories directly in my current profession. I do want to caution everyone here, that if you start your journey only looking for the financial value, you will more than likely disrespect people at some point, thus rendering the entire effort short lived and destructive. Focus on your culture and your people and the dollars will show up.

Think about how valuable a company that people love to work for and enjoy pouring themselves into can be. I am seeing that kind of culture in pockets where I am now. I dream of a time where it is not in pockets and it is rampant throughout the entire organization, that is the goal for me.

I am going to start by giving some additional insight and slight recap to the work I do. I am now completely focused on Lean and Continuous improvement as I mentioned in the Chapter on my Journey. I work within a 650+ Project execution team that is part of a 4,500+ person energy company in the United States. My role affords me the privilege of working with just about every single department in the company, but the bulk of my work is within the Project Execution Team. That team starts with a commercial business opportunity to transport, process and deliver natural gas and other energy projects. There are project development folks, project managers, environmental specialists, construction managers, contract specialist, project controls, Land agents, surveyors and engineers as well as lots of centralized support services within the team and spread across the country. The work is to design, contract, and oversee the construction of new assets as well as improvements and maintenance projects on existing assets.

As I begin to sit down and think about how I want to structure this chapter, I have to be honest and say I wasn't sure. The part of me that is excited and interested in getting this book out now, is saying, take the easy route and go in chronological order. I can easily sit down and write things out in the order they happened for me. Heck, that is just a rewriting of my "to do" list. Pretty easy. I had to take myself back to my goal of this book and where I think the value is and the easy route isn't going to get that done. Therefore, I am going to start with the most impactful stuff first and somewhat disregard the chronology of it all. For those that set reading targets based on finishing chapters and get some reading retainage fatigue as the chapters wind on, you will appreciate this approach. I may have experienced the aforementioned reading experience a time or two in my life.

When I think about the most impactful use of Lean in my work it is very easy to realize it has to be the thing that had the biggest impact on people. For me, that was Process Mapping. As I type that I still struggle to believe that is true, but it is. The Process Mapping work that I have undertaken has allowed me to use many Lean tools and principles. It has also had a very tangible impact on the people involved.

Full disclosure here, some of the groups were not "onboard". In some places there were some major cultural hurdles to overcome, and I think that is why I put this first and feel it had the biggest impact. Process Mapping removed some of those hurdles. As the Team Lead, Team Member, Sponsor or in most cases the Facilitator I was putting my passion for improvement and respect for people on the front burner and turning the heat way up. Even more transparency, some folks really didn't even get it after we built the process maps. It took some time to see it in action and shift the culture.

This is a great time to talk about some of the very real benefits I have seen from Process Mapping. I again am going to list these in order of importance as opposed to the order they typically happen. First, engaging the actual people who do the work in defining their process in a very structured and visual way gives them ownership. That ownership translates into confidence, pride and a really important word that seems to be missing a lot in today's society; accountability. I have found that if people are engaged and empowered they are more than willing to accept the accountability. They also care more about what they are doing. I can guarantee people who care more about what they are doing are more effective and get better results.

Next, is flexibility. The fact that there is a simple visual way to show what needs to be done allows for flexibility of resources. An individual from another functional team that has the capability and skill set can jump in and help someone from another group that may be struggling or having some time constraint issues. Process Mapping allows flexibility to shift individuals in from other teams to provide resource support as well as not losing a step if someone leaves or gets promoted.

Another key benefit is being able to visually and simply identify when, where and with whom communication needs to happen. This is extremely critical as all Lean Continuous Improvement needs to be considering the full value stream and the customer requirements within that value stream. The single biggest hurdle to understanding customer requirements is communication.

So why is that such a hurdle? I have found that most folks don't even know or understand who all of their customers are. They may have an idea of who is next in the process, but it is very easy to lose sight the further down the value stream you go. A Process Map really helps mitigate by visualizing all of it. I have also found that even when teams identify who the customers are it is not always transparent when they would be engaged, what else feeds into the product they are seeing and what they might actually care about. The Process Map is a very efficient and effective way to show the connectivity of different steps and what the full package may look like by the time its gets downstream. It also allows a mechanism to start talking or thinking about the types of metrics or value that is added for the customers. The visualization can really help you identify or prioritize things like cost, schedule or quality.

You can take any customer requirement and roll it up into

one of those three categories. I always hear what about safety? That can fall into any one of them. If something is not safe it doesn't meet the quality requirement. If something is not safe it will likely cost you more money and finally if something is not safe it usually causes schedule delays. At this point I want to touch on something I have heard in the past. The Project Management Triangle, cost, quality and schedule. I have heard many times, you can't have all three, better quality will cost you more money and so on. Some folks say you have to pick two. HOGWASH! You can have all three and I have seen teams get all three many times. You can guess which tool I have seen provide all three; a correctly developed, well defined Process Map. I know of one specific case where I circled back to a team that never had a Process Map. They developed, implemented and used Process Maps for about a year on a number of projects. Those projects cost millions of dollars. When asked how much of an impact the Process Map had over those projects the answer, I got was 20% better. I said, "What was 20% better, the cost, schedule or quality" and the answer I got, without hesitation was, "All of them"!

Another impactful story I have around Process Map development is around education and awareness. Once the maps were developed and implemented, they were placed in highly visible and accessible places, such as the walls of the rooms where team project meetings were occurring or on the walls in the common workspaces where most of the cubicles were located. I was standing near one of these areas when someone I was not familiar with engaged me to ask if I was the one to hang these maps up? In that conversation I found out that the individual did not work within any part of any of the process maps hanging on the wall. They were, however, a key downstream customer of the final product of the overall process. What was said next was very eye opening for me and very impactful. They were completely shocked that there were so many steps, hand offs and complexity to get to the final product they were seeing. They were interested in one Process Map in particular and were blown away at all of the research, legal and documentation work that goes into completing their particular task. This awareness turned directly into positive behavior as they went directly to one of the individuals in that process and said, "I had no idea you had all of these steps and I guess I shouldn't be so picky about some of this stuff." Seeing the big picture in a visual and easy to digest manner created some respect, appreciation and additional consideration that has a lasting impact on that team.

Now that there is visualization and consistency in several areas, those areas can really start to leverage the power of Lean. One of the many things that a process map helped with that I have to tag as the next biggest impact item is Voice of the Customer. **A Customer is anyone or anything that consumes all or part of something you produce.** I made that bold because the pure Lean definition of a 'Customer' is not only important, but I find myself going back to it often. When folks aren't sure where to look downstream for customer feedback or requirements, I pull this definition off the shelf and when it is applied against a Visual Process Map it inspires all kinds of thoughts. We have had great wins with Voice of the Customer work on meetings, reports, milestone deliverables and final product deliverables.

Being able to identify who those folks are has been a key first step and is not always easy. I can confirm without a doubt teams that have some process visualization; a Process Map or simplified version called a SIPOC are far more successful at knowing where to go for customer feedback and therefore far more successful at meeting the customer requirements. If you are a leader in an organization adopting a Lean culture or you want to be, making sure your team knows who the customers are, what their requirements are and if those requirements are being met is part of your scope of work.

I want to dive into SIPOC for just a minute, as for teams that have trouble seeing the value in a Process Map; usually because they don't want to invest the time in building one. The SIPOC is a powerful tool. It is a very visual tool, just like the Process Map, but takes a much higher view of things, generally taking less time to populate. I have seen several teams start with a SIPOC, see the value and then transition to a Process Map. The SIPOC tool is a visual diagram depicting the **S**upplier, **I**nput, **P**rocess, **O**utput and **C**ustomer. This would be done for major milestones or deliverables but not every task. Five to ten P's has seemed to be the sweet spot for most teams I work with. You start with the P, by listing the first major milestone or deliverable in the Process, you then move left to the input you need to do that and then all the way left to who supplies that. Your next step is to fill in the output of the step and the Customer of that Output. This order and visualization is very powerful to show the evolution of your overall process. It also very clearly shows you the output and customer of that output; providing a visual hint to where you should be looking for customer feedback and gathering data.

When it comes to Voice of the Customer you really need to understand that it should be documented, when you get it, who gets it, where you put it and what you do with it. You also need to remain aware that these requirements can change and therefore needs constant attention and adjustments. I have seen teams do this extremely well and seen others struggle with it. I can tell you the teams that understand Voice of the Customer well have kept it simple to collect and have showed good correlation of the actions from the feedback with key business metrics.

Another key Lean tool that I have seen flourish is Structured Problem Solving. There are several key methods to do this and I am not going to dive into them all. The key take away is that any method of Structured Problem Solving you use is going to require you to define the problem with data and re-measure the problem after your potential countermeasures are in place. You must have an apples-to-apples data set to compare to your original problem statement.

I have applied structured problem solving with many teams on many different issues here with incredible success. Most issues hit on more than one type of metrics, cost, quality or time, but they have all had clearly defined impacts on at least one of those, or we did not invest effort in going any further. If none of those things were being impacted, we could make an informed decision to go look at another problem.

That was the case on several different issues that have come across my desk. Any problem is a perceived problem until you can gather data to confirm not only that the problem exists, but how big the problem is. Utilizing Structured Problem Solving has saved us tons of time and effort and allowed us to focus on investing our time and effort into problems with impacts that outweigh the effort to fix them. I have many examples of Structured Problem Solving projects that saved us Millions of dollars, weeks of cycle time, days and hours or re-working defects, and eliminating defect to reduce risk.

One key thing I can note about these efforts and sticking to the rules on Structured Problem Solving is the implementation and the sustainability of the improvements far surpasses anything done without this methodology. Starting at Step 1 of clearly defining your problem (the gap) with definitive data that can be re-measured, then setting improvement goals from the data with the team that is experiencing the defect creates a very high level of respect and engagement. Both are key factors in a viable countermeasure being implemented and sustained. If there is no respect and no engagement and only edicts coming down from above, the teams will only change when someone is looking, if at all.

This seems like a good time to talk about how we have used waste reduction and elimination as it ties in well with the Process Mapping, Voice of the Customer and Structured Problem Solving. Several teams have taken on very serious Waste reduction and elimination exercises and have been very successful.

The aforementioned Lean tools have all provided ways to identify potential waste. Once the potential waste is identified and the proper lean tool or principle is applied we have seen the waste shrink significantly or disappear altogether. Some of the biggest success in the Waste reduction arena is around meetings and reporting. Like many big companies we spend an insane amount of time in meetings and preparing reports. WASTE!

There have been several efforts here to collect data on the non-valuable time in meetings and non-valuable portions of reports that has saved thousands of man hours per year. This has been done by first collecting data on how much waste there was in those activities. Then analyzing that waste and applying potential countermeasures. The real power was in re-measuring after the potential countermeasures were implemented. This proves the countermeasure works and has allowed folks to share as a best practice with others experiencing similar waste. The re-measurement has also provided clear data and inspiration for folks to keep going and dive deeper. Most teams find some quick wins, then use the extra time and energy to go even further. Some of the things that have changed is the format and cadence of reports and meetings, automation of some of the redundant tasks or information, utilization of automated reports with good, intuitive visualizations to reduce the status updating in meetings and flat-out cancelling things that aren't helping.

Further on waste reduction and elimination. We have seen Millions of dollars in cost reduction by eliminating or reducing waste in our processes of executing capital work as well as in our contracting for materials and services. Once again, the areas where we have seen the biggest impacts are where the teams are leveraging Process Maps, Voice of the Customer and Structured Problem Solving tools. These tools all bring the waste to the surface as well as clearly spell out the full value stream. It is very important to understand that if you see something as potential waste you need to first know the full value stream. What you may perceive as waste may be incredibly valuable to someone else downstream. If you eliminate $100 worth of waste in your world and it has a $1,000 increase elsewhere you are doing it wrong.

When we have taken the proper steps to identify potential waste and understand the full value stream we have had major wins that are sustained years and years later. There are lots of examples where certain tasks were being performed that brought no value, or data collected that brought no value and by analyzing the impact of not doing those things and confirming no negative impacts they were eliminated or adjusted when they couldn't be eliminated fully.

Some of these improvements simply required taking something off of the Process Map or out of a scope of work for an outside provider. Some of these were more complex and required finding a new way to do things. This is another spot where metrics and re-measurement are very important. Some of the potential waste reductions that were tried didn't work the first time and needed to be revisited multiple times until the desired results were achieved. Without good metrics and sound re-measurement the target would have always been moving and the teams may have never gotten to a viable solution.

I can think of one such waste identification and reduction

effort that analyzed old contracts that may have been written in less favorable market conditions and when older technologies were being used to execute the work. A discussion ensued about what has changed since these contracts were written 8 years ago and what adjustments can be made that don't negatively impact the value stream. The findings provided a saving of over twelve million dollars per year that we are still realizing today.

Another great example of Lean impacts at work is Visual Management. Whereas a SIPOC or Process Map are forms of Visual Management there are many others that have had a great impact in my work life. A great example is when the common practice used by Project Managers of holding project contingency became a problem and the behavior needed to change there was simple, intuitive visual management developed that showed the status of the 'new behavior' and the impact it was having on the bottom line. That information was hung up everywhere. It was displayed in common areas, such as in the community kitchen on the refrigerator door and on the back of the stall doors in the bathroom. In a very short amount of time the way folks behaved around contingency drastically shifted and resulted in millions of dollars of savings on capital.

The Kitchen and Bathroom became a beacon for Visual Management. Any behavior that needed to change was hung in those areas, such as cost and schedule predictability of projects, safety metrics, environmental stewardship metrics and defect metrics. All items quickly moved towards the desired results in large part due to the Visual Management.

The visual management examples can go on and on, so I will just mention briefly some of the unique and/or highly impactful ones. There has been effective visual management used to communicate Voice of Customer data on many occasions. To take all of those numbers, pair them down to what is important and then visualize them in an intuitive, sometimes fun way has made engaging and energizing teams to address gaps in the customer requirements much easier. As I mentioned earlier engagement is key. Using Visual Management to share our Customer Data has helped produce many impactful improvements around the organization.

Visual Management has also been used to provide key safety reminders. We work in a dangerous industry and things like complacency, ignorance or carelessness has no place. There was a string of safety concerns that while none directly impacted the health and safety of the individuals involved, they were all very close to being extremely impactful. This was around picking up large items and them swinging out of control and coming towards and through the cab of the equipment. In all cases the operator escaped injury. Some of our field teams engaged in adding some Visual Management to the cab of the machines that would do those lifts. The photos of what things looked like after the mishaps, being placed in those cabs, where the individuals operating the machines could see them, provided a powerful, visual reminder of what could happen if you are not following all of the procedures and aware of your hazards. There are lots of similar examples on the safety front.

Another Visual Management tool also ties into the very profound concept of tracking your KBI's is near miss reporting. Not only were near misses reported, but visual management started to circulate widely with the results. The Near Misses, which came from those reports are calculated into a ratio against the actual incidents that happen. Goals were set, which at first were met with a lot of questions and frustrations as they seemed extremely difficult to achieve. In a very short amount of time those numbers moved closer and closer to the goal and within two years far exceeded those goals. The importance of the issues; the why, as well as the well placed, accurate, intuitive Visual Management shifted the culture quickly and effectively.

The other areas where we are seeing great success with Visual Management is in waste elimination and reduction. By providing simple, visual intuitive ways for folks to display not just the waste they are looking to reduce, but the status of the effort groups remain energized and informed around the efforts. It is really powerful and refreshing for folks to be able to see right in front of them, that someone listened and they are doing something about it. Some of the boards that are out there have a little fun, using dumpster icons or rain clouds, or smiley faces. Allowing teams to engage in the Visual Management in a fun and entertaining way provides a nice break from the day to day as well as some much-needed inspiration.

So many processes are completely inundated with waste that both the break and the energy are desperately needed. In this area I always encourage teams that are new to this to start small and build up. Go back and review the sections where I mention Paul Akers if you need to know more on why that is important and how to do it. He is the master.

In this part of the chapter I am going to talk about a couple of Lean tools and principles that are similar, but different. I have seen lots of folks get these things confused and create some hurdles. For those that really understand the difference and leverage the correct concept or tool at the correct time, the results are impressive. I am talking here about Gemba Walks, Go and See, and Management by Walking around. The key difference is the structure. A Gemba Walk is going to observe and understand a specific process, with a defined scope where the work happens. There is a start and an end to what you are looking at. The other two are more informal and the focus is on the individual and the relationship, everything is on the table, how are the kids, what's for lunch, what processes are broken. I do think knowing the difference is important. You must ensure all parties involved know which one it is.

I will start with a Gemba walk. When I first learned this tool I was hesitant to go and apply it. I am a problem solver and now I am being told no solutions, go observe, ask the right questions, empower folks and inspire them to fix the problems or ask for help. I am not going to be there to see something go wrong and tell them how to fix it? Sounds like a challenge for me. I took the training again, mostly because I had no confidence I could do it right. I really trusted the person teaching it and knew I had to be missing something. I felt far more comfortable, but still not ready after my second go around with the training, so I was invited to go along on a Gemba Walk as a shadow.

I was very fortunate that the person leading the Gemba Walk is a strong leader, cares about his people and did a very good job. Just a couple of minutes into the interaction everything clicked for me, a major ah-ha moment. A good Gemba Walk gone bad can be extremely damaging to your culture, your relationship and your business, so if you aren't sure, go watch someone who does them well; extremely valuable use of your time.

As Gemba Walk became the Buzz Word and the organization began to wildly push them down as goals for managers, several folks were becoming soured to them and were not looking forward to them. If you are a leader and you are doing Gemba Walks well, your team will be happy to hear one is happening or better yet, requesting one to be done. I have witnessed this firsthand. Talk about engagement and energy, here it is! Imagine calling your leader up and saying, "Can you come Gemba Walk this process"?. As a leader you should not only be focused on properly and effectively performing Gemba Walks, but you should be correlating that effort to how many hurdles are being identified and hopefully, ultimately removed.

One of the biggest arguments I have heard against Gemba Walks is that they are too formal, too structured and I just want to be part of the team and build relationships with my people. Great, I strongly encourage that. Respect for People, I can't say it loud enough or often enough. You can get out there in a less formal way and develop those relationships, call it a Go and See visit or Management by walking around. These are extremely powerful tools and can drive absolutely amazing business results, but it is not a Gemba Walk, so do them all, just know which one you are doing and make sure everyone else does as well.

The simple differences in the three different methods is: A Gemba walk has a specific scope in the space and time that it normally happens. GO and See Visits are observing whatever happens to be going on that day and Management by Walking Around is strictly relationship building, no work or process, things like kids, or sports, get to know the team personally.

I want to spend another minute on the Go and See visits. I have had the privilege of working under several Senior Leaders in my career that were absolutely amazing at this. Not only did they take the time to stop by and chat, they found ways to make it meaningful. As an example, a CEO of a 2,500 + person company walking into my office when I sit five levels below him in the org chart asking me very specific questions about me and my dog; his photo was on my wall. This created an environment where I would run through a brick wall to make that man look good; make the business look good. It may sound like small beans, but there are dozens of those stories from dozens of people here and the business results in the areas where those stories are told most often are incredibly impressive.

I am sure that I might have missed some interesting Lean

tools and principles here, I know I have used 5S, Poka Yoke and spaghetti diagrams to make improvements, but these are the key ones that have been used multiple times, brought value and continue to keep showing up as options for other improvements. You have to keep in mind, we do not manufacture anything, we are designing, building and operating energy assets, so applying something directly from the Toyota world as a direct copy is not an option. Yet, I still find myself filled up with activity and never starving for ways to apply Lean.

LEAN IMPACT ON PERSONAL GROWTH

Personal growth; what an interesting topic. I tend to think of myself as an others first kind of person. I take joy in serving and providing for others. With that being said, why would I apply Lean to Personal Growth? To myself? The answer is simple, a better me can better serve others.

I profoundly believe in that train of thought and am supremely confident I live my life accordingly. I sometimes slip in this area and lose focus on my personal growth, on myself. I very quickly realize others suffer because of this. I am so intensely focused on helping others improve that I quickly see my lack of focus, energy, drive or patience is extremely damaging and really hampers my ability to help others. I have been getting progressively better at catching this and have made more timely adjustments. Those adjustments usually start with me thinking; pump the brakes get focused on you and right the ship. Guess what I use to do that? Lean!

It is hard to find a single bigger impact and source of value than applying Lean to my own personal growth. The way I have grown as a person has been nothing short of amazing. I think in my gene pool and the culture I grew up in, there is a little hard headedness, a little resistance to change and a little "old school", as they say. There is some incredible value in that and there are lots of things I apply those inherent traits to, such as discipline, work ethic and morals. I am and will remain hardheaded and resistant to change on those things. However, I am changing and growing and will continue to change and grow in most other aspects of being me and Lean is the key to that happening in an effective, efficient, and most importantly sustainable manner.

As I provide thoughts and examples on utilizing Lean in my personal growth, I will start with Time management. The first Lean tool I applied was visual management. I started very simple and kept expanding the complexity of my system as the value increased. I simply started by visualizing my 'to do' list utilizing a color-coded system. If it was in the 'Red' column on my list it was a 'must do' and has the highest priority. The yellow column is the 'should do' stuff and the 'Green' column is for 'nice to do stuff'. Other than listing the actual thing that needs done in the proper column I would also list the estimated time to complete the task.

I operated this way for quite a while and there is no doubt it helped me get more done, and not miss important items, all while lowering my stress levels. Documenting, visualizing, and having a plan for all those things running around your brain does wonders for reducing stress levels. If this is the only thing I did on this front I would still be sharing it, because it was very impactful and helpful for me and I would want others to enjoy the value.

I did however, kick this thing into high gear and took it to a much higher level. Improvements are continuous to my 'Planner' and I never skip filling it out. There were brief periods of time in the past when I felt 'too busy' to complete it. The way I felt and the things I missed getting done have conditioned me to never miss again. I am not sure on exactly how long the streak is now, but my guess is I am approaching 2 years straight of filling in my 'Planner'.

Some of the key Lean changes to my 'Planner' over the years are around data tracking and evaluation. It wasn't until I started tracking what percent of each category I planned and checked off that I realized what a 'Red' actually was, recall those are the 'Must do' items. When I first started tracking and analyzing the data I was missing a very large percentage of 'Reds'. This was a real eye opener for me.

If I am missing this many 'Reds' how am I 4still successful, improving and surviving? If they are really 'must do' items, then I would be in a whole heap of trouble. Trending the data really did help me learn what a 'red' is and now far less items make it into that column. Those that do; get done. I am happy to say I recently had a 10 month stretch where I completed every single Red. Ironically, after I felt like it has been a long time since I missed one, I went back and confirmed the 10 month streak, the very next week I overloaded my reds and missed 2 out of 7.

I am updating my monthly and yearly data sets for how many I had planned and how many I checked off for each category. As you can gather from what I just said about my 'reds' a very high percentage of those got accomplished. For my 'Yellows'; the 'should do stuff', I am usually between 75% and 85% each month, with 'Greens' dropping down to usually less than 50% and sometimes even 0%. The 'Greens', since they are 'nice to do' are usually more fun and recreation type things. The months I get zero Greens, I usually move some of them into the 'Yellow' category for the following month. You have to have some R&R.

This whole system is built around visual management and driving ideal behaviors, which drives ideal results. Using visual management and most importantly the data has provided me a very reliable way to target where I need personal growth attention and sometimes even help from others. I certainly have not been able to close the gaps that the data was showing by myself every time. It has assisted me in reaching out to friends and family for their help.

This tool has become such a part of my life and so critical that I carry it with me more than my phone or my wallet. I have expanded it well beyond time management and in doing so made some of my biggest strides in personal growth.

The first, highly impactful thing I did was add visual management around what a good day means to me. I was inspired here by the Jim Valvano, don't give up, don't ever give up speech. In that speech he says if you do these three things you had a pretty good day. Those three things are laugh, think and cry. He felt if you do those every single day, what a life you have. I don't disagree with him and understand it to be true but didn't see that as my exact list of what makes a great day, so I came up with my own and made a clear inspiring way to display them on my 'Planner'.

I chose to put them there because really good visual management is at the point of use, and I use nothing more over the course of a day than my planner. My list is 'Exercise

Patience', 'Focus on Persistence', 'Display Leadership', 'Lead with Humility' and 'Be a Light'. All things I care about and all areas I needed personal growth in to become the man I want to be.

This visual management spring-boarded me into breaking out another Lean concept of Voice of the Customer. That may sound crazy, but it has and is paying huge dividends. I started to think about why I seek personal growth and who are the customers of that growth? The simple answer is to be a better husband and father. The rest is great, and I certainly see growth benefiting other things, but those are the key areas. Once I established my Value Stream, I engaged those down-stream customers for some feedback.

If I truly am seeking growth in those areas and my wife is the downstream customer of my husbandry and my children are the downstream customers of my parenting, then I need to know if I am meeting their requirements. I take those 5 key, every single day behaviors and at the end of the year they rank me 1 to 5 on each of them. This is done in an anonymous fashion to help create psychological safety, especially for the kids. It is pretty easy for my wife to tell me where I need improvement, but this can be a challenge for the kids, so I do my best to give them comfort.

The first year I did this, you could tell the safety may not have been there, or maybe they didn't understand the value of honesty and a low ranking is something I needed to improve. I was not wanting to see all 5's. There is no room for growth if I have all 5's. They did deliver and my lowest ranking category was 'Exercise Patience', followed closely by 'Be a Light'.

I pivoted quickly and began working on those gaps, starting with 'Exercise Patience'. The first thing I did was increase the font size on my visual management. Exercise Patience now jumped right off the page. I also added a metric and a monthly target for catching myself being calm and exercising patience in a situation where I otherwise would not have. I did set the bar pretty low at first, just one a month, but moved it up quickly until I was documenting 5 or 6 a week.

On the next biggest Gap, 'Be a Light' things were not so easy and straight forward. I was struggling with those results. I thought I was doing pretty good on that one. The patience one would have been the one I would have laid money on, and I am not a betting man, but being a light? I am a light, how am I lacking that self-awareness? After some discussion it circled back to there was some uncertainty around what it meant.

The Lean wheels immediately began turning. I had to document and visually manage what this meant. To me, things I am being a light for are the things people can follow. People look to the light, people follow the light. I had to sit down and list out what I want to be displaying with a goal of people following it. So the list was made and it became another visual management box on my Planner. It also got hung in the kitchen for everyone to see.

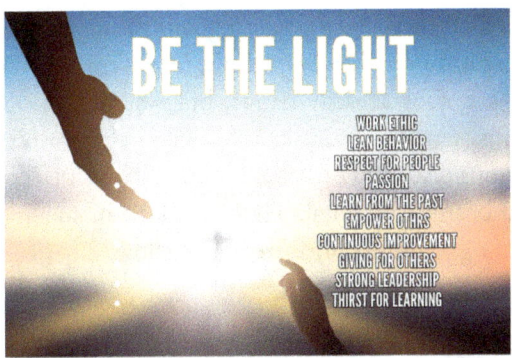

This whole concept and approach also really displays another key principle in Lean, show what good looks like. The 'Be The Light' List and the planner are both very valuable pieces to showing my family what good likes like when it comes to a Lean Continuous Improvement effort on personal Growth. There are lots of pieces of these things they are now utilizing to help bring value in the areas they want to grow.

The results showed up. I moved the needle slightly on the patience front. I moved the needle all the way up on the light front and secured almost all 5's on that behavior. I could make the argument that as it relates to personal growth, moving the needle on 'Being A Light' had the biggest impact. I have a list of ten behaviors including things like respect for people and work ethic, so the fact that others can and do look to me for what good looks like in those areas is very, very important. I am very pleased with how that is working.

Another personal growth needle mover I applied some Lean principles to, utilizing the 'Planner' is developing good habits. This one has some overlap into the later chapter around lean health, but also has several general personal growth items on it. What I did is establish a list of 17 daily habits driving personal growth as well as good health. Some of those habits were already in place and pretty basic so they went in as 'Red'. Others were becoming habits, maybe weekdays I was doing it but weekends I wasn't, they went in as 'Yellows'. The ones I want as daily habits, but was not even close to being consistent with went in as 'Greens'. This wasn't done in the columns discussed earlier as it would have cluttered up the tool and been detrimental. These are done in small boxes on the lower right and are organized by the flow.

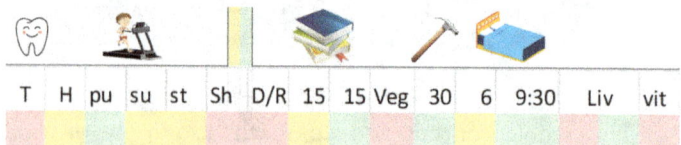

Flow is very important in Lean and organizing things based on the most efficient flow makes it much easier, and faster to get them done. Another benefit of organizing habits, or aspirational habits by a logical flow is helping you build the new habits by habit tethering. Habit tethering allows development of a new habit, by connecting it to something you are already doing. As an example, if you want to develop a daily habit of reading for 30 minutes, you can start by reading 5 minutes directly after something you are already doing every day, like brushing your teeth, or having a morning coffee. You then can incrementally climb up to the 30 minutes you are seeking.

I have found myself improving here but have a long way to go. It did seem with the visual management, flow and tethering that I was going to knock it out of the park and be doing all 17 things every single day. I was getting around 12 right out of the gate and very soon was in the 15 or 16 range. I was feeling great and about to pat myself on the back for an amazing win and huge step in personal growth when things somehow turned around real fast and I found myself complacent on many of the desired habits. This was frustrating for me as I know I felt so much better the days I got 12 or more checked off.

What I did is leverage the data and increase the visual management. Instead of just checking them off each day and throwing the planner out at the end of the week I started tallying the check marks each week and accumulating them for the month. The visual management shows me a week-to-week comparison and the total for last month, inspiring me to improve on a month-to-month basis. I am also placing this data on my monthly recap section, which is a journal type entry that I keep for each month that also houses my 'Red', 'Green', 'Yellow' percent complete data. I am now using the habit check mark data to correlate with some of the positive and negative tone of my journal entries for the month with a high number of checks and a low number of checks. If the data can clearly show, the more checks the better the month, I should be inspired to be more diligent.

I know it seems like this chapter could have been called the 'Planner' because everything revolves around that. Everything revolving around one tool in is Lean. Almost everything that needs a gap closed I am able to manage in one single place and a place that I engage with continuously. I do however have another tool utilizing lean concepts to drive my personal growth. The two actually do interact with each other and things from one may show up on the other.

Several years ago, I developed a really good habit of journaling. I do this at a minimum of once a month and 13 times a year. I will do more as needed. Those numbers are kept on my 'Planner', so journalling may move into the 'Red' column as the end of the month nears, if I haven't done it already. I use this journal to pour out my thoughts, good and bad. I also use it to plan and make inspirational statements, as well as just getting some stuff off of my chest.

One thing I found is a lot of the getting things off my chest quickly turned into writing down what I plan to do to change it. You could call those action items. I found I was coming up with great action items, but not following through. As I was writing one month, I was struggling with something I knew I wrote about prior. When I was done I went back through my old writings and found it.

Enter my Lean mind. I immediately went into the writings for the entire year and kept a tally of anything that was an action item. I then tracked how many were completed. The data is significant to say the least. I had 47 action items over the course of the year and only 16 of them were completed. Talk about waste. All these great improvements and nothing is being done with them. I immediately began to underline any action item. I also kept more real time data and started adding 'Journal Action Items" to; you guessed it, the 'Planner'.

The very next year I ended up with 54 action items, 50 of which were completed and 2 more completed shortly after. There were only 2 of 54 not acted upon. Still room for improvement, but a massive improvement over the prior year when 31 of 47 were untouched.

The next real big area where Lean has made an impact on personal growth is in the structured problem-solving arena. More specifically around problems we were having with kids' behaviors. There were certain frustrating behaviors causing pain points. We began to document and track these to define the problem. We then worked with the kids to set a target to close the gap. Using root cause analysis, we came up with suggested countermeasures. We then got visual management in place for the re-measurement data as well as the proposed countermeasures.

We did this on whiteboards, in the kitchen where everyone could see them. The results were amazing. Not only did we close the gap, but we understood better what makes each of us tick and what some of the not so clear contributing factors were to the bad behaviors. We are no longer using this tool and are also very rarely experiencing those pain points. I am not claiming perfection because that is not our goal. Kids should still be kids and have some leeway to make some mistakes to learn from, exercise some of their creative thought, and expel some energy. If the frequency of things not aligned with our expectations increase too much we will not hesitate to pull out a fresh whiteboard and get back to it.

Another Key Lean component proven to provide incredible value in the personal growth area is having system aim. This is one of Deming's key points and I was given the inspiration to charge down this path by a great Lean Mentor and friend. He coached me through creating a meaningful, metric based Mission Statement. The Mission statement ended up being two simple sentences, but it was no simple journey to get there. Trying to establish a mission for your life that is valuable, impactful and measurable requires a great deal of thought, personal reflection and self-awareness.

Here is another area my unquenchable thirst for Lean Learning crept in and provided the solution to my struggles. I mentioned Paul Akers earlier in this book, as an amazing beacon for Lean. In one of his videos he spoke with Ken Mogi about his book, "Awakening your Ikigai". The book is great, and the talk was insanely inspiring to me. It gave me a tool to start mapping a path to a mission statement.

I actually created an Ikigai board for myself. I took the Ikegai diagram Mogi shared in the book and transposed it onto a whiteboard, so I could brainstorm and visualize the different components overlapping. Ikigai is an Okinawan custom that means your reason for being. The components making up Ikegai are; that which you love, that which the world needs, that which you can be paid for, and that which you are good at.

I keep this diagram on my wall still and in the whiteboard format. I would expect some things may expand or new things may be added, as I grow as a person, develop my skill sets and adjust my system aim, hopefully to a position even higher than I ever thought I could be.

My current Ikigai Diagram.

The items visualized on the diagram provided great inspiration and direction on what my mission should be. Once I had a clearer picture on my reason for being it became easier to see my mission. I took the information

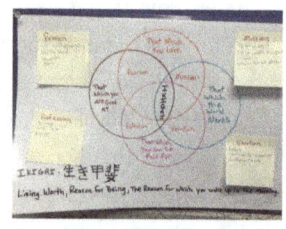

and boiled it down to something I wanted to strive for tying into my Ikegai and measuring it. After a couple of iterations and bouncing it off of several folks I now have a clear personal mission statement with associated metrics. I have a system aim.

So, who cares, you may ask. I certainly do. The folks who are part of that mission, since it is based on helping others, certainly do. And those that interact with me certainly do. There has been lots of value showing up on this front and I don't know how I got by without it. Perhaps, most impactful is my stress levels. I have far less stress in my life now. Pretty impressive considering I have far more stressors in my life now than I ever had.

Here is the simple thing that the Personal Mission Statement has done to diminish my stress. If something happens, I simply ask does this impact my personal mission? If the answer is 'No' I quickly dismiss it, thus not culminating and building stress. Some things linger, but it is very rare anymore. If the negative input, or potential stressor coming in does impact my personal mission statement then I make a plan to address it. I have to address it if I want to achieve my mission. It is amazing how much stress can decrease on an issue if you have a plan, even if the plan is to deal with it later.

I learned from a wonderful book by David Allen, called "Getting Things Done". He provides key resources and concepts to help anyone get things done. He shares 2-minute workflow, which has been highly successful in lowering my stress levels. Anything you get, an email, phone call, text, conversation is an input and running that input through the flow allows your mind to get rid of it, until you are ready to do something with it, if an action is indeed required.

The basic idea is if the task takes less than 2 minutes, do it. If it doesn't you need to decide if it is actionable. If it is not, you get rid of it or store it for reference. If it is actionable, you get it into your task management system. A key thing you need to do here is not just add the task, but the first action.

This allows your brain to move on from the task and not have to use any precious brain power to think about that task until it is time to do something with it.

The impact; the value that applying Lean to my personal growth has had on me in substantial, sustained, ever growing and has affected lots of other people in my sphere of influence. It has been contagious, and I am extremely happy that it is.

Lean Impact on Health

Health is essential for our existence. It affects everything from how we feel and look to how much energy we have and how long we live. No matter how healthy we are, there is always room for improvement. I fluctuate on this. I have times of incredible positive progress and I have times of complacency. I know I can do better. How about you? Can you improve your health? Can Lean help? It has for me.

A great Lean practitioner that I mention several times in this book is Paul Akers. Paul has two very interesting and impactful things; his book, "Lean Health" which I talk about a lot in this chapter and a podcast series where he highlighted another author Ken Mogi and his book finding your Ikigai. I mentioned Ikigai in the prior chapter as well. I want to get something in front of you at the beginning of this chapter about Ikigai. It helps you live longer! How about that for value!

When I think about the application of Lean to health it is easy to establish a direct connection to my previous chapter on personal growth. The two are very connected and many of the same tools and principles responsible for fueling my personal growth are also fueling major improvement to my health. I spoke a lot in the prior chapter about stress reduction which is a key to being healthier. I will focus in the chapter on other items that are not directly related to stress reduction.

When I think about health there are some key metrics, like weight, blood pressure, cholesterol, etc. I had some issues with all of those over the years, prior to my Lean journey escalating. I also want to touch on other benefits of Lean that may not be as tangible or evident as those numbers that most people are familiar with. I consider things like how much energy I have, how tired I feel doing certain activities and how much pain I experience when trying to be young again. Those things are not as tangible and not as easy to measure, despite the lack of empirical data, I know I have improved in all of those areas since I started applying Lean to my health.

The first real epiphany for me was reading Paul Akers' book, "Lean Health." He has so many great points in there and I adopted many of them. At the basic core of it, I get my steps, I do pushups and sit ups and I get the majority of my calories from fruits, vegetables, nuts and good proteins like fish, chicken, pork and eggs. I by no means have been as diligent in this as Paul has, but I also have not seen the extreme results he has. I am down around 40 pounds, have less pain and more energy, but do not have the very cut physique that he does. I am very confident if I followed everything in his plan and strategy to the tee, I could achieve that and maybe someday I will, but for now I find value in generally feeling better and stuffing myself full of ice cream once in a while.

As I instituted a lot of what Paul was sharing in his book on top of more energy, less pain and my weight dropping some other key numbers improved greatly. Initially, my blood pressure was borderline high and is now very solid, right where it should be. My cholesterol was also too high for what doctors recommend for someone my age and border line being told to take medication for it. I am now just slightly above the ideal target, but well within what most doctors consider healthy. Perhaps the biggest thing that shifted for me is the Iron levels in my blood. I have a genetic disease that causes my body to retain iron instead of keeping what it needs and getting rid of the rest like most people. The disease untreated can be extremely dangerous as the iron starts to settle in your vital organs and once settled can't be reversed.

I am constantly getting lab work drawn and yearly ultra-sounds of my organs. Once my iron increases past a set number I have to go into a treatment center and have a bag of blood taken out. This can be very annoying and sometimes slows me down the day it is taken and the next day. There was a stretch of time where I was going in every two weeks for treatment. I keep metrics and visual management on not only my lab numbers, but my contributing behaviors and treatments. My doctor is always impressed with the data I have and the way I show it. This is a way I applied Lean directly to something very serious that impacts my health in a major way.

Back to Paul Akers, when I started his program, I noticed my iron numbers not escalating as fast and, in some cases, coming down without a treatment. I was completely shocked, as was my doctor. Through applying Lean tools like structured problem solving, gap analysis and Key Behavior Indicator metrics it was evident the shift in lifestyle towards the Paul Akers Lean Health model was the single biggest impact. The results started to show up in the first two months, and by six months in were undeniable. I now get treated 3 or 4 times a year. I also tend to only stick to the Paul Akers program about 75% of the time. If I can ever get rid of some bad habits and move that number close to 100%, I am very certain my frequency of treatment can improve even further.

Before I get further into Lean impacts on Health, I would

like to float this out there for anyone reading this book that might have an idea on this. The blood they take from me is thrown out. The Red Cross does not accept it. As far as I know the only thing wrong with it is that is has too much iron, which for lots of people with serious injury, surgery or battling cancer, Iron rich blood would probably make them feel much better. I would love for someone smarter than me to figure out why that blood must be thrown out and if there is a way to salvage it and help those in need. Right now, the bi-product of my treatment is waste (blood), that I hope could be repurposed.

As mentioned earlier, visual management is extremely impactful and can drive desired behaviors very efficiently. Health and Fitness is no different. There are several visual management applications that have proven very effective.

At a very high level, a simple visual management board on how often you exercise can really help drive behavior. Like any other visual management this has to be in a spot that you see it and it drives the behavior. For a long time that spot was next to the mirror in my home gym. This really helped me increase my workouts from once a week to 5 or 6 times a week. The tool has a box that lists some simple workouts and is labeled once a week. It also displays an image of someone who likely doesn't work out or at least not more than once a week. The next box is 2-3 times a week and has similar information and an image of someone slightly more in shape. The last box is 6 or more times a week and has an image of Arnold Schwarzenegger in his prime.

I also have a little sticker with my name on it and the first time I get into the gym for the week I place it on the diagram where I ended up the prior week. I spend a lot of time in the 4 and 5 day range, which is decent, but not the pinnacle. The power of this tool really showed up the first time I had to come in and put my sticker under the guy in the first image. I got really motivated and made it to the Schwarzenegger zone for the first time ever the following week. This tool still proves valuable and I still kind of use it, but have found a flaw in the system. I am experimenting with a change.

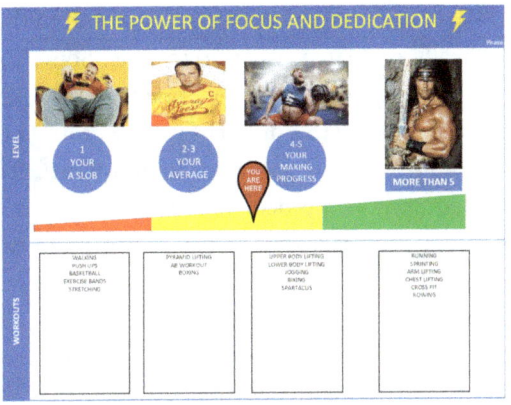

The tool worked great to motivate me to get in the gym the next day, but was only visible if I was in the gym. I had some hip pain and was taking a break and not getting into the gym at all. It was during this time that I found the flaw. If I don't see it, the behavior doesn't ever show up. I am trying different locations for it now, like in my clothes closet, which helped a little, but still misses the mark. I may add it to my Planner.

Another use of Lean for my health is in visual management for diet. On the inside of the pantry door, I made a document that has foods in there that help me written in dark green over a green background and on the other half foods that hurt me written in dark red letters over a red background. As I am about to take something from the pantry, I have a very lean reminder on the impact that item will have on my health. I still pick the red thing once in a while, but nowhere near as often as I once did.

Another area that Lean has improved my health is by attacking the waste in my individual workout sessions. It can be very difficult to find enough time to get into the gym and make it count. If you only have a short amount of time to invest in the gym you need to ensure you are not wasting a lot of time. I have been able to apply my Lean mind to this in lots of ways. I really evaluated my waiting time. Some things are too intense to go right from one exercise to another, or sometimes you need to move to a different muscle group. I thoughtfully plan out what I am going to do and when. I consider things like equipment needed, muscle group impacted and focus or energy required. Once I have all of those considerations in mind, I generate a plan that minimizes the waiting or resting time.

Through applying lean thought to improving the flow of my workouts and reducing my waste I made and continue to make changes to where the equipment is in my gym. I am constantly evaluating where certain pieces of equipment are placed and which equipment needs to share plates, or which exercises need a timer. I don't see this process ever ending for me. As I change focus areas or make adjustments to rest certain muscle groups I constantly adjust my workouts. I always have the flow and efficiency in mind and that has helped me really maximize my limited time in the gym.

Another principle I employ as it relates to my health is visualizing my 'Why'. I sat down and put great thought into why it is important to maintain a certain weight, or stay in control of my iron, or bring down the blood pressure and cholesterol. I listed out my "Why" utilizing strong visual management. I kept it simple and to the point. I utilized colors to help make it jump off the page.

I have a list of items that I want to do written bold in Green; some things like set a good example for my kids, have more energy and even some purely measurable things like sub

6-minute mile time (I was under 4 minutes at one point in my life), or fitting into an old suit that I used to love to wear. On the other side of the paper I have written out things that I don't want in bold red letters. This side has things like; die young, have to buy new clothes, be in pain, among others.

This 'why' exercise and furthermore, the visualization of it has really helped me in times when it feels much easier to eat the entire bucket of ice cream and watch a movie as opposed to cutting up some fresh vegetables and going for a run. It sure isn't perfect. I certainly still find myself eating the entire bucket of ice cream and watching a movie, but nowhere as often as I once did. I also don't feel so guilty when I do have those moments, because there is a proven plan in place to get back on track.

Lean at Home

People spend considerable time in their homes. They invest a lot of money. We love our homes, so why not make your time there as valuable as possible?

There are a lot of ways Lean can apply to the home. Everything at home can be more pleasing if you take 'Leaning out' your home seriously. I can certainly appreciate that you may be concerned about applying this business mentality at home creating a work / life balance issue, and I get that, but don't buy it. If you have something great going on in your life and if you are doing this right, it is great, why not want it in all aspects of your life, work and home.

I used to say the phrase work life balance a lot. I was focused on it at one point, but now it is just balance, no separation and I am much happier approaching things this way. I want all the work wins to turn into home wins and vice versa.

I was able to apply Lean really well in the time management arena for work and I would argue the time at home is far more important than the time at work, so it needs to be managed more diligently. I applied the same visual management tools to the overall time management at home. Inside of the tool, "My Planner", there is capacity for prioritization, allowing me to really get home time where it counts the most.

I also use 'My Planner' at home to drive desired home behaviors, such as coffee or a walk with my wife, or specific activities with the kids. All of these have visual real time targets for day, week, month and year.

Another sort of time management at home was gathering cycle time data on my morning routine, then setting targets for cycle time reduction that required process improvement. The first thing I did was eliminate the tasks that were not wanted. I made huge strides in this and reduced a 2 hour and 10-minute process to just over an hour long, all while still doing everything I wanted. I managed this with a white board and analyzed cycle time at a very granular level. With this data in hand, I attacked not just the order in which things were occurring, but also the process of doing them.

As an example, starting to make my eggs while my tea was in the microwave utilized the time I was waiting for tea for progress on something else, making eggs. A process which has sustained many changes. One in particular, I used a specific burner on the stove, and I found myself dripping some egg on the stove on my way from the pan to trash can causing me to clean it up and waste time. I moved to the burner directly next to the can and now crack the egg and get it into the can without any mess and more importantly no clean up time.

Another great improvement coming from the Leaning of the morning routine was no longer batch processing dirty dishes. We were great at letting them pile up and then investing a chunk of time to get them rinsed, into the dishwasher, then put away. The new process is real time, single piece flow. The dish gets washed dried and put away as soon as its use is over. We slip on this sometimes, mostly at dinner since we try to eat as a family and one of the contributions the kids make to the harmony of the household is clearing the dinner table, which currently creates a batch of dishes to process. I do, however, adhere to the single flow dish process the majority of my one-off meals or snacks.

Another improvement opportunity at home is our communication as a family. We dramatically improved this by implementing a Huddle Box format, which we intended to use weekly. This does not currently happen every week due to lots of conflicting schedules, but we try to do it as often we can and really make it a priority if we know there is a lot of stuff coming up.

We sat down as a family and decided on what is important to check in on; these became the huddle boxes. We stick to these boxes and it really helps us be efficient. My wife and I can sit for a longer period of time planning and talking, but the kids grow tired of it, so being efficient is key to keeping everyone engaged. The boxes we landed on are Progress made, which is where each person talks about any key progress made on something they were trying to accomplish since the last time we talked. Next, there is a box for something fun or something that belongs in our family memory box. This is a spot for each person to share those things that brought them joy. I am always touched to hear how many times someone's else's success makes it into another person's box on this one. As an example, my one son saying something for the memory box is his brother hitting the game winning shot in a basketball game. The next box is for things happening this week. Here we can share what critical things are coming up that others might need to be aware of, things like travel, medical appointments, big projects at work, key assignments at school or tests. This section is where we can really help each other out and offer some direct help, or indirect help. As an example, since you have a big project for work this week, we will take Tuesday night and go do something. That way you will have some focus time. Or the simple question for anything school related, "Do you need help with that"? Which often is followed with a Yes.

The last box is where everyone has a chance to add anything they are concerned about, for the week, the month or the year. This has really allowed us to get ahead of some things and work as a team on some bigger more complex issues that we may not be individually equipped to handle. We have set the expectation that you can leave any box blank if you don't have anything for that topic. We typically finish the sharing and understand what each of us needs to do to help the others be successful in under 15 minutes.

Another key thing that we sometimes, not always include in the family meeting is a teaching moment. We rotate these and each person takes a turn teaching the family something for 5 minutes. There have been some really amazing topics and I have been blown away by the quality of the presentations from my kids. We have had some very profound and impactful topics, like active listening and emotional intelligence.

Another impactful use of Lean at home is visual management. I have listed lots of examples in prior chapters, most of which are in the home, so here I will focus on the ones that are directly related to the family dynamic and what is going on in the home. The previously mentioned planner is a huge part of the day-to-day operations around the house, maybe the single biggest thing that makes thing go!

Outside of that we have visual management in place for the kids' chores. The chore boards are pretty simple, very intuitive and not only shows what they should be doing each day, but also displays right next to the actions the earning potential for the different responsibilities they have. The more they do, the more money they can collect at the end of the month for their chores.

With a successful Lean culture as a guideline, we engaged and involved the children in the chore process. First, we involved the kids in the conversation around what chores they are doing and when. We check in on this fairly often and have made several adjustments over the years. This also grew as they realized they were not really being challenged anymore and they could use some more money. Next, we involved them in deciding how the chores will be communicated and tracked. Just like the chores themselves, this evolved over time, and we keep checking in on what is working and what isn't. Finally, we cover chores in the last family meeting of each month. We review what was done in the prior month, including us paying out for it, and we talk about what chores are coming up and where they have concerns about getting them done, if any.

While we are on the topics of kids and Lean we have success by working together on small white boards that identify behaviors that are expected. This process was great and created some interesting and valuable dialogue. Not only did the process create opportunities for us to teach the kids, but also woke us parents up to some of the perspectives and challenges they have that we did at their age. On these charts we list out things like what time they need to be home on a weeknight, a weekend, where they are allowed to go without informing us or asking permission and also some more serious items, no alcohol or tobacco, or vaping.

Along similar lines a couple of summers ago the boys started the break from school off on the wrong foot and their behavior was far from acceptable to us. We sat down with them and listed out four specific behaviors that were not aligned with our expectations. At that point we asked if it was fair for us to ask them to do better on those items, to which they agreed. We had a good dialogue about what they needed to make those improvements and made it crystal clear that we are not demanding perfection but are demanding improvement. We worked together to establish consequences for lack of improvement and built a system to track the progress. It ended up being a simple visual that had an up or down arrow based on how they performed on that behavior that day. My wife or I would put them on the board each night and we tracked how many of each there was each week and each month. We tracked progress; fewer down arrows is the goal. There were consequences in place for every 3 down arrows and for weeks that the number of down arrows increased.

This process and tool worked amazingly well for us. We really did grow much closer through the process and their behaviors rapidly improved. Within six weeks we stopped filling in the boards because the arrows were always up.

If you are well versed in Lean you are more than likely using "5S" at home and we are as well. For those that don't know what that is here you go; Sort, Set in Order, Shine, Standardize, and Sustain. This took a while to get cooking in our house, but once we got one room behind us, we set targets to do one a month. It has since slowed, since we added a new component to the process that requires more time and money. We have adjusted our goal to eight rooms or areas in a year. We follow the same process for each room or area, so I will layout the general process.

The first thing we do is take absolutely everything that can come out of the room out. Anything that is garbage gets thrown out immediately and not moved around or staged anywhere. The rest of the items get laid out where everything is visible, not all piled up on each other. Next, we clean the room top to bottom, which is much easier when it is empty. As we give the room time to dry or air out after the cleaning, which would include shampooing carpets in a carpeted room, we evaluate all the stuff. Anything that we don't NEED in that room gets designated to be given away or sent to where we do NEED it. The next step is to measure the room out and draw a detailed, to scale diagram of the room. We then use that diagram to plan where the things we NEED are going to go. This step usually requires us to budget and plan for some purchases, like shelves, bins or boxes. We are very thoughtful about this. We plan shelf sizes based on the bin size, so everything fits very efficiently.

In the process we have also somewhat standardized the types of bins we are using, clear with a lockable lid. Even though we label the bins on 2 sides, so it is visible regardless of orientation, we found the clear bin allows you to see what is inside as well as if it is full or not.

On the diagram we sketch in the new changes, such as shelves or bins and we hang the diagram in the room as a go by. This has helped sustain the change as well as cut down on the time we spend looking for stuff.

The part we added that has spread these efforts out is decorating the rooms. Neither my wife nor I have a strong passion around the fluff. We love to see it and appreciate others that have lots of fluff and wish we had more fluff, but neither of us have stepped up and made it happen. So now, as part of our planning we identify the functional purchases, the bins and shelves, but also the fluff, like a nice painting or decorative item. This usually requires more time and always more money, therefore a room a month is not going to happen for us.

We recently improved this whole process by engaging everyone in deciding the rooms to do and the leadership responsibility changing. We each get a turn to pick a room and whoever picked the room is in charge of coordinating the work and keeping things on schedule and budget. This has been a great teaching and learning experience for all of us and creates a nice team environment. You tend to work harder even in the room you didn't pick, so that it can get done and the team can get onto the room you want done.

I could probably write an entire chapter about some of the cool things we came up with during this process. Things like each person having a specific color laundry basket that goes in a very specific spot. Sock bins for everyone's socks so the effort of pairing socks is shared, you take care of your own. Another is the simple fact that if I want to clean something there is a portable carrier that has everything I need. It also has a spot, and that spot is directly under the refills for the cleaning supplies.

Another Lean influence that has improved things in our home is how we manage construction improvement projects. We do this very visually and collaboratively. We start with everyone creating a sticky note for anything they would like, such as a new deck, or a putting green. On the sticky note you add a single dollar sign for something under $500 to complete, double dollar sign for projects that will be $500-$1500 and a triple dollar sign for anything over $1500.

We then have a white board with sections under each dollar category for primary project and secondary projects. We set some basic guidelines based on our budget for the year. As an example, we may say we can handle two of the most expensive, three of the mid-range and four of the lower end projects. We then each take a turn to put a sticky note in the primary project row, until all of those are filled. Once that is done the rest of the sticky notes go into the secondary project category.

On the diagram we have a box in the bottom right for completed projects. It is extremely satisfying to move a sticky note into that section and is really nice to see this section filling up as we get closer to the end of the year.

Much like the Lean room projects each family member takes the lead on certain projects. You become responsible for making sure everyone knows what needs to be done next and doing the work or getting help to do the work required to complete the project. The high-level steps are visualized in one place and provides an effective way to communicate everything going on. The more complex projects we develop a more detailed schedule, list all the steps and setting some milestone target dates as well as budget check in point.

The last example I want to share for the home speaks directly to value and utilized structured problem solving and visual management. The value was our church needed parishioners to dig a little deeper and contribute more for items that came up. We were currently contributing and were also running very close on our monthly budget, so something had to be cut. We decided to cut electricity, so we did the cost per watt calculations and identified some of the biggest offenders, like leaving a computer on while not using it. Our particular computer at our rates was $480 per year of waste. There were others.

The board showed those big ticket items as well as our reduction in usage over the same month in the prior year. The difference in the cost is the extra we gave to the church every month and was highlighted on the board to serve as motivation.

We were able to provide additional funds to the church every single month that we did this. All while keeping our monthly budget intact. We simply eliminated some electricity waste and converted that into Dollars for the church. The one month we actually sent in an additional $198.

LEAN SPORTS

Improving, winning, breaking records, making money, becoming immortalized; all things that can be desired and achieved in sports if you want.

This area is not only where I get the most energized and have the most fun applying Lean but is has also helped me get attention from those nay sayers that are stuck in the "We don't manufacture anything" mindset. I have leveraged results and stories from the application of Lean to move lots of people off the Lean fence.

When I first started thinking about how to apply Lean to sports, I instantly became energized. I love sports. I love competing and love getting better at sports, almost any sport. I mentioned earlier in the pre-journey chapter some Lean behaviors I was displaying as it related to sports, before I even knew what lean was, so I will focus this chapter on when I decided to make it more formal.

As with anything Lean, applying it to sports starts with respect for people. When you think about what that means in sports it's a very interesting dynamic, as a coach part of your job is to guide and direct. I have found and firmly believe that it is very possible to guide and direct but also empower and engage.

I have a couple of thoughts here based on my experience. One of the things I really had to put on the front of my mind is that everyone on the team is trying to help that team win. It is extremely important to communicate the intention of why you're out there and to understand the players' intentions. You need to help make sure everyone is aligned. I think it is important to do this through clear and concise goals that are visualized and developed collaboratively with the team. Since I've been involved in youth sports, the number one goal is never winning. There have always been other things that are far more important in the development of Youth and Sports. We do list winning on the goal charts but usually somewhere 4th or 5th, not at the top.

By involving, engaging, and empowering everybody right from the beginning you're showing respect. When people especially kids feel respected, they're going to contribute more and they're going to give more effort. One of the things you should be doing as the coach/leader is to gather, understand, and clearly communicate the requirements to meet the goals that were established by the team or organization. As the leader you need to ensure that you are empowering those players and removing those hurdles that keep them from achieving the goals.

Also, along the respect for people front, I always engage the team in the solutions to close the performance gaps. As an example, the kid out there trying to stop the other kid's team from scoring has a pretty good idea of why the other kid keeps scoring and it's not because he wants him to.

I have been able to successfully work with lots of athletes on applying Lean in basketball with multiple teams at the youth level and even the junior varsity level in high school. I've also been able to leverage lean with my son and his high school golf career. Other areas where I have seen Lean applied include; high school baseball, motocross racing and competitive archery.

The youth basketball story starts with me showing up to a youth basketball meeting for my older son, who was in fourth grade at the time. I played some basketball in my life and had some really good experience to share but had never coached anything or even thought about coaching anything. Based on my basketball background and experience they asked me to be the head coach for the fourth-grade travel basketball team.

I somewhat hesitantly dove in and decided to just play it by ear and see what happened. My first approach was to just take some of the basic drills I did in high school and college and have these kids do the same thing. I quickly realized I didn't remember absolutely every drill and more importantly the order in which we did them. I had to go back to the drawing board, and I decided to start leveraging some of my lean background to improve how we practiced the fundamentals.

I started with simply creating a number and letter system to help organize everyone and everything. There was a series of A's and a series of B's that went one through six. We had twelve kids that first year. Just having those designations allowed us to move more swiftly through our practices and get much more accomplished in our limited time together. The other thing we did was to standardize the fundamentals part. I knew from the beginning that I was very passionate about making sure these kids developed the basic fundamentals. I listed out with another coach what we thought the most important fundamentals are. I then spaghetti diagramed them, making sure to designate what drills needed cones, balls, partners etc. By doing so we were able to streamline the activities and minimize the time we needed to get set up with cones or get balls. These drills reinforced the fundamentals and were consistently ran every single night; still are.

I have a very interesting Lean minded note related to the standardization of fundamentals; we kept cycle time. The end of the second line drill marked the end of the fundamental session and moved us on to what we all thought was the more fun and enjoyable part of practice. The kids really challenged themselves to get that first part done as quickly as possible. It is important to note, by done it doesn't mean that you just checked it off, it meant that it was done correctly.

To make that happen we had to very visibly put out there a lean principle of knowing what good looks like. For each and every drill we walked through in great detail what it was supposed to look like and what it was supposed to improve. They all knew what good looked like for every single fundamental drill. They weren't allowed to move on to the next drill until that first drill was completed correctly.

We kept the cycle time record for this portion of the practice on a little white board and when the last kid would finish his line drill, they would usually ask what the time was. They were very engaged in trying to reduce that cycle time and get on to the other parts of practice. The first time we ran the drills it was almost a full hour. This was somewhat frustrating, but I knew it was important, so we just pushed forward. Somewhere in the middle of their 6th grade season they had reduced that cycle time down to 9 minutes 16 seconds. That was their record when they left the youth program. I found it very enlightening that not only were they getting it done substantially faster, but the quality was incredible. Every drill was being done at the highest level, exactly how it was expected to be done in a shorter amount of time.

So, to recap on the fundamental portion of our practices we were able to leverage a spaghetti diagram, standard work, knowing what good looks like, cycle time, flow, and most importantly respect for people to bring incredible value.

Next, I want to talk about the impact of Lean as it relates to converting what's happening in the game to what we're doing in practice. The first key point here is leveraging a gap analysis tool. After each game and especially in a league game when we're going to play that opponent again, we as a team completed a gap analysis diagram. That diagram showed the current state which was the score of the game we just completed. It also showed desired state. The team came up with that collaboratively.

Within that there is an offensive and defensive component. The team would come up with how many less points the other team should have scored had we done everything well. They also come up with how many more points we should have scored had we done everything well.

That data is then broken down into offense and defensive root cause analysis. The team, not the coaches start talking about what was the root cause of us not scoring enough points. This continues until there are no more ideas on where there were opportunities for us to score more points. This is also done for the defensive side. What caused the other team to score more points than they should have?

The next step is to take each and every root cause and ask for countermeasures. Again, we are asking the actual players that played the game. In this portion it is important to note that there certainly can be more than one countermeasure per root cause. These countermeasures become some actions that we can take at practice. It is important to note here that as the coach you are the expert, and therefore if there is something glaring missing you should ask the right questions to try and drive them to that answer.

I was very concerned in the beginning that this was going to be a big issue, as the athletes that were going through this exercise the first time were only eight years old. Much to my surprise, the coaches had to add very little if ever anything to their root cause or countermeasures. I firmly believe this contributed to kids learning and understanding the game much faster than they would have had we just been there dispensing solutions.

I want to share what was perhaps one of the most profound moments during our gap analysis. This will provide an actual example of how what I explained works but also some incredible thinking by a young child.

Directly after the game and during a root cause analysis breakdown of why the other team scored more than they should have an athlete identified they often beat us down the court. This was certainly true as the other team did score a lot of transition points in that game. A recommended counter-measure provided for that root cause was running more line drills at practice. For those that are not familiar with a line drill, most athletes absolutely despise them, it is a running drill that can be pretty grueling if you take it seriously. The first time I heard that countermeasure I had to pause and look at the athlete and say, "Are you sure you want to do more line drills?" and their response was, "If it helps us win".

Another insightful and impactful moment for me during the gap analysis was a root cause and counter measure that had come up multiple times. As we went through the exercise one of the athletes raised their hand and said "coach, haven't we tried that before? Shouldn't we try something else?" I wish corporate America could embrace that type of thinking, we tend to be more bullheaded and not open minded about trying something different. A side note to this story, I told the kid that I was really impressed at how intelligent that was and he must get great grades. His response, "not even close coach!"

I want to share some results from this Gap Analysis exercise. As I mentioned earlier, we were very diligent about doing this for league opponents who you play more than once. I now have 18 examples of the same teams playing again in the same season. 17 out of the 18 were extremely close the second time to closing the defined gap. The one that wasn't we were missing a key player due to injury.

The first one ever that we were able to compare was at the 3rd grade level. We had lost the first game by two points and during the gap analysis it was identified by the players that we should have won by three which was a five-point swing. The second time we played that team, two weeks later, with four practices in between, we won by three. During those four practices we really did focus on the countermeasures that the athletes came up with. If they recommended more line drills, we did more line drills. If they recommended, we needed more time running our offensive plays we did. If they recommended more shooting drills, we did them.

At a youth level where winning is not my top priority, improvement is, this tool has been incredibly impactful. Every single time the tool was completed the goal was improvement, which sometimes meant winning, but not always.

The next lean tool I want to talk about on the basketball front is visual management. Perhaps one of the most impactful visual management tools was the goal card.

One side of the card listed out the team goals developed by all of the coaches in the program. The other side of the card left room for each kid to list out some personal goals that they wanted to achieve. We encouraged each kid to take a shot at creating those goals. We then worked with each one of them one-on-one to refine those goals to be something measurable.

Once those personal goals were set we laminated that card and gave it to each kid to put on their basketball bag. This put the visual management of what the goals of the organization were as well as each kid's personal goals in a place where they would see it constantly. We also checked in with kids on their personal goals as well as the team goals. We asked a lot of questions, like are you achieving your goal? What is in the way of you achieving your goal? If they answered that they needed some help we tried to block out some time to help them.

There were lots of other ways that we utilized visual management with the basketball programs. Some of them were season long others were very short to address a very specific need. When you think about visual management for sports, you should be thinking about visually managing those things that are worth knowing. You should be showing whether you're achieving your desired results or not. You should also show if you're exceeding your desired results or short, and by how much. If you want to shift behavior, all of this needs to be visual and most importantly intuitive. If you need to be standing there to explain what it means it will fail.

Some of the things that we use visual management for, other than goals, were KPIs like reducing turnovers, increasing assists, cycle time of fundamentals, shots made during shooting drills, and cycle time of speed drills. When you think about visual management for sports or anything else it's important to understand that it really must be intuitive, it also should be as close to the point of use as possible. It needs to be simple and up to date. The information you are showing needs to be current. Most importantly and I cannot stress this enough; it must drive the desired behavior without producing any negative results elsewhere.

Those items were the most heavily leveraged lean tools on the basketball front. We did however use other lean tools, such as Kanban to show where we were on some of our larger gaps or initiatives. We used common boards to display some of the bigger opportunities and highlight areas of focus based on the information coming in from the athletes. Another lean tool we leveraged from time to time was huddle meetings. We used this structured format at times when we needed to communicate a lot of information very quickly. We set the goals for those meetings, established those boxes, and most importantly stuck to it.

As lean is so heavily ingrained in everything I do, I'm sure I may have missed a couple of things. These items mentioned are the most impactful and critical ones that we leveraged. As I mentioned, this started in the youth program and was brought along with me when I was asked to coach at the junior varsity level. The applications and results were very similar at both levels.

Also, I have been able to influence the varsity coach and use a little bit of this lean stuff with the varsity team as well. One key item that I used with the Junior Varsity team that Varsity adopted is utilizing a Key Behavior Indicator (KBI). We built a tool that documents winning behaviors and losing behaviors that might occur during each play. You can have multiple positive and multiple negative plays on every possession. We worked with the varsity athletes to define what are winning plays and losing plays. We then asked them to watch their game film and come up with cumulative scores of winning and losing plays. This was highly impactful and drove the desired behavior. It really did help the athletes understand little things that were happening during the course of a game that had a major impact. We saw a drastic increase in the net score of every player who took this seriously.

I now want to move into how lean was leveraged for golf. My son is currently a junior in high school. He has been playing on a school golf team since 7th grade. Going into his freshman year he was nervous about being able to make the varsity team. I asked him what he thought about leveraging lean principles to try and increase his odds. He was all about it and took it very seriously.

The things he leveraged and is still leveraging are visual

management, standard work, KPI's, Gap Analysis, and structured problem solving.

With golf, much like basketball, the number one priority was improvement. Winning was also a goal, but not the top priority. He has now completed three full seasons of leveraging these principles for golf. The improvement and the winning have been incredible. The team has won their first conference championship in almost 30 years. My son was also the first individual sectional champion from the school in that same period of time.

Much like basketball it started with visually displaying team and personal goals. Those goals were displayed on the first page of a small book that was kept in his golf bag and he utilized during every practice and match.

Another highly impactful place that visual management was leveraged is on the practice range. One of the issues he identified during practice is that he was just out there ripping balls into a wide-open space. He knew that to improve his game he had to be more focused and dialed in on hitting an actual target. To do this, on an letter size sheet of paper he created a visual of a red and white target. He would set that piece of paper directly next to the basket of range balls during his practice. Every single time he went to get another ball he would see that visual management reminding him to aim for a target.

The next tool being used was standard work. He leveraged this in multiple ways. First was his pre-shot routine. He understood how important consistency and muscle memory is to a golf shot. So, he established what he felt was the best way to be ready to take a golf shot. He documented this and listed it in the book I mentioned earlier. He also realized that the routine was different for a putt and a regular shot, so he documented both. As this firmed up and he saw the value of it, he decided it needed to be part of his practice routine as well. To help achieve this he added the words pre-shot routine to the visual management target I mentioned earlier.

The other area where he used standard work is his pre match routine. He works through those items that made him feel the most prepared for a match. This involved the way he hit on the range, the amount of time he hit on the range, the way he putted on the practice green, and the amount of chipping he did. As with the shot routine he documented this and followed it. This is a piece of standard work that has had many revisions over the years. As an example, when the need for him to improve his putting became evident, he added more putts and time to the putting green and less to the driving range.

Another way he utilizes visual management was on the psychology front. He is a very fiery and competitive kid, which can create some struggles in a sport that requires focus and calm. He recognized that his frustrations and anger were leading to an increase in strokes. So, at the end of each round in his book, he would list two or three bullet points on what he needs to do better and then very intentionally underneath that list the things that he did well. This method allowed him to understand where he needed to be better, but most importantly had him end on a high note. He was now leaving the matches with the last thing he thought about being what he did well. This helped him be calm and focused.

Another visual management and psychology trick that was used during short periods of extreme stress and frustration, was using a blank sheet in that notebook to write down everything that he was angry or frustrated about in the round of golf. He would then tear that sheet out and very intentionally rip it up into small pieces and throw it into the trash can. This was his way of physically connecting to his brain that the bad things are over and behind him.

The next lean principle in golf is KPI's. He sat down and listed out those things worth measuring that drive the desired results. Those are things like fairways hit, greens in regulation hit, putts and score. These KPIs were kept in the same book that I mentioned earlier and readily available during a round or practice. These KPIs clearly showed current state and desired state as well as the gap.

With a solid KPI system in place, gap analysis became the next logical step. After a round he was able to analyze these KPIs and make decisions around where the work needed to happen at practice. As an example, if his score was higher than he desired, and his biggest miss was in fairways hit he could dedicate more time on the range to the tee shots.

Lastly, he uses structured problem solving. This philosophy is leveraged on the courses that are played multiple times or key events like a district or sectional tournament. Knowing that this course and event is critical to the success of himself and the team he took extra steps to analyze every shot he took. He used the same book and for each hole and every single shot he documented desired state versus actual state. In many cases the desired state actually met the current state, so he would Simply put a check mark.

Where that was not the case, he would document what the shot was and what it should have been and what that impact would have been to his overall score. As an example on the first tee he hit his hybrid off the tee and it landed off the left side of the fairway. The desired shot there would be the same distance but on the right half of the fairway. He felt that would have produced a one-shot reduction in his total score on that hole. In the match he shot a bogey on that hole. He feels that is a parable hole for him. He does this analysis for all 18 holes, every shot. He then looks at the ones that should have been different and trends that information.

In this particular match most of the trending was on the tee shots. This allowed him to do a couple of things. First invest more time on the range in his tee shots. Which includes using different clubs, it is not always going to be a driver on this golf course. The trend also let him know that he needed to be thinking more about which club he was hitting off the tee and making sure that he was making the right decision on clubs. This particular event is one that it is easy to see the value of lean. As a freshman he finished 22nd and shot an 88. As a junior he won the event with a 76. It is important to note that the 76 came on a very cold very windy day where it was sleeting and raining, not something you can account for in the structured problem solving. I do believe the score would have been even lower had the conditions been similar to his Freshman year.

I'm constantly sharing the successes and stories of Lean and sports. This is absolutely the area where I am most energized and excited to be leveraging these things I've learned. There have been many instances while sharing these stories where people have asked me to help out with the sports that their kids are playing. I have now been able to provide insight, guidance and some tips for teams in softball, motocross racing, and archery. It is amazing how most of the tools I talked about that were focused on how we improved basketball and golf are easily relatable to these other sports.

When I think about the impact and value that lean can bring to sports, I wish there was more information out there. Earlier in the book I mentioned the New Zealand All Blacks rugby team. The book by James Kerr, "Legacy', shares a lot of information about their culture and how they use lean. I would imagine if sports weren't so secretive and competitive, that there may be other books out there about how other organizations are using Lean. I can't help but watch how the New England Patriots and Bill Belichick operate and not believe there is some Lean influence and background there. I have also heard rumblings that Nick Saban at Alabama is versed in Lean and a lot of what they do follows Lean principles and practices. I wish I had some definitive information here and could learn from it, but for now I will just watch what they do and understand that it is Lean, and it is bringing value, as those organizations win at a very high level.

I almost feel like I could write an entire handbook or guide on how to apply Lean to sports and provide lots of the examples that I gave earlier more tangibly. Maybe someday that will make it onto my radar screen?

Lean in Religion

Religion, now that is an interesting place to think about continuous improvement. Most religions have been around for thousands of years and little has changed. In this chapter I'm going to give some examples of where the church I belong to has utilized Lean continuous improvement, and also examples of how individuals can use Lean to understand and increase the positive impact of religion.

First, I'd like to set things up a little bit just by explaining my religious experience as well as my overarching thoughts on religion. I was born and raised in the Christian faith. For the last 20 years, through my wife, I have been actively involved in the Catholic Church. Therefore, a lot of my thoughts and examples are going to be based in the Christian faith.

I do, however, think that the same principles and concepts apply to any religion. As I firmly believe all religions possess a common goal of believing in a higher power that helps to guide behaviors, morals, and ethics.

When I think about applying Lean to religion, I feel very fortunate that the current Catholic Church I am attending has a priest that embraces this, and another very active parishioner that worked at Goodyear and has a Lean background. I want to share some very tangible examples of Lean in our actual church.

First, and I use this example often when people ask me what does Poka Yoke mean? Poka Yoke, means mistake proofing. Making it impossible to do something wrong can sometimes be difficult to provide examples of. I always go to a great example that was utilized within our church. Our dual-purpose gymnasium slash banquet hall requires a lot of setup and tear down of chairs and tables. The carts that are used for the chairs need to be stacked in a very specific way for the chairs to not fall. This has been done wrong many times. The first countermeasure that was put in place was to put a diagram showing the proper way to stack the chairs in the closet where the chairs are stored.

This did create some improvement; however it did not eliminate the problem until they took the next step. The next step was a Poka Yoke. On each cart one chair was zip tied to the cart which made it impossible to put the next chairs on incorrectly. This countermeasure has proven to be really effective as we have not seen a defect since this was implemented.

Next, I want to talk about commissions. There were commissions formed for lots of different topics such as building maintenance, worship, and education. These commissions formed and developed goals, a system aim. The commissions leverage many Lean principles over the course of their existence. These committees tend to be very successful when there are strong facilitation skills in place. Also, many of them utilize visual management tools.

Some things that are visually managed are the goals, the organization, and specific gaps they are trying to close. As these commissions set forth on their goals they are collecting data and using lots of visual management and other tools to analyze and share that data. Most of these commissions are extremely data-driven. With the data in hand they could easily identify where the gaps are as it relates to their system aim. They are then taking on different initiatives or applying different countermeasures to try and close those gaps.

All of these commissions roll up into an overarching structure. That structure has a system aim for the entire church. The manner in which these teams are operating and reporting out displays lots of Lean characteristics.

The commissions have gone a long way to empowering the masses, the rest of the parishioners. In a lot of these types of organizations it seems that a few are tasked with all of the decisions and all of the work. In this model a lot more people are getting involved because they're engaged, empowered, and understand the system aim.

Another thing I want to share about the commissions is a day long event that was conducted that reminded me an awful lot of a rapid improvement event in Lean. Everyone was brought in and there was a keynote speaker that delivered an amazing speech about praying with your feet. That session served as an inspiration to get everybody thinking about the system aim of the church. There then was a small breakout session that drove engagement of all the attendees. After that everyone was broken up into small groups and talked about what hurdles might exist to achieving the system aim of the committee. Those hurdles were then pick charted, which places them in relativity to each other based on the effort to complete it and the impact it would have once completed. All of this was done on large pieces of flipchart paper and very visual for all of the other groups to see.

I want to share one thing that really opened my eyes and I have used other places since. I typically leverage questions to get teams to drive towards system thinking. I have several in my back pocket that I pull out as needed. The questions asked at this event were a different approach and I really like it. It really did change the way my brain was thinking about Root Cause and Countermeasures. Each team was asked to write down what the committee looks like in 20 years if it was successful. Then were asked to list what changes were made to get there? Then why where those changes made? To me, this line of questions reverse engineers things. It starts with the System Aim, makes you think about a new current state and then the countermeasures put in place and what root cause was present that required those countermeasures. A unique approach and one that worked very well with the audience.

There are several other ways that Lean is being leveraged throughout the church. Many of these could be used at home as well. One thing that was done was an analysis on the consumption of energy for the lighting in the church. It was determined that the payback period to switch all of the lights within the building to LED was worth the effort. As that massive project was undertaken it was performed in a very lean manner. There was a lot of thought put into not only the process of swapping the lights, but which rooms would be done when and in what order to make it more efficient.

Another thing being done around the building to make things more efficient is landscaping changes. These changes are all focused on making things more efficient. Some of the planting areas that used to become laden with weeds and required weeding are now matted and covered with decorative rock, much lower maintenance on the weed front and also does not need replaced every year like mulch. Also a lot of the shrubbery that was difficult to maintain and didn't provide much aesthetic benefit has been removed. The shapes of the landscape beds that remain as well as some of the other items that remain have been set up so that they can be easily mowed around from a riding mower, making things far more efficient.

The last thing I want to talk about as it relates specifically to my particular church is voice of the customer. As the committees have formed and everyone has started to move towards the system aim this has become a critical piece. There's constant feedback being solicited at different events. This is done through in person conversations, online surveys, and surveys completed with the assistance of helpers.

It was evident when voice of the customer really started taking off that there exists a lot of diversity in how people want to provide feedback. There are lots of people that would prefer to not speak to you in person and answer through a computer survey. There are others that do not like working on the computers and struggle to get through some of the links and some of the functionality. They would much rather sit with somebody and talk through it and fill in their information. As surveys are conducted now this is considered and most, if not all are done through multiple channels.

This focus on voice of the customer has provided many wins for the church. First and foremost, it has increased the engagement of most of the parishioners. Secondly, it has brought in different perspectives and uncovered things that otherwise would not have been uncovered. Finally, it has generated changes that impact the entire system, brought forth by those within the system.

I now want to pivot and talk more philosophical and about leveraging Lean outside of my actual church. I have been able to glean an incredible amount of value from my church experience over the years. I really want to share that, without being overly churchy or pushy. I know that doesn't work for everyone. In my experience, some of the people that need the value church can bring the most do not want to hear anything about church. As I began to evaluate how I can make this valuable for them, I had to really think outside the box.

What is interesting to me is where I've seen traction here is just discussing the value. I share the value that I am getting and what it means to me, then start asking questions about the value that others would want to get not only from church but from life. As those answers come flooding in, and they typically do, I can easily point towards something within religion that helps provide that value. I will caution that I have to be very careful in doing this and sometimes just ask the right questions to lead them to the answer as opposed to giving it to them.

This also means that sometimes to soften the blow I need to try and disconnect it a little bit from religion. When I say disconnect I mean making things more like symbolism as opposed to hard and fast rules or beliefs.

An example of that relates to heaven. In a deep discussion about religion with someone who I thought needed to find some value in religion, the topic of heaven came up. There was not a strong belief in an actual heaven as most people think of it. So, when I asked, "what is the point of heaven and what is the value of it", their response was to help guide the right behaviors here on earth. I tend to agree with that. I also firmly believe the concept of heaven helps us that are left behind to cope when a loved one moves on.

I then began to focus on that value of the right behaviors here on earth and how to drive them. What are those things that could move this individual towards those behaviors? I know there are people very close to him that he respects a lot. Unfortunately, several of them have passed. I started asking questions around what they would think if they were still here. That seemed to really strike a nerve. I then asked what if heaven was just your memories and thoughts of those people and wasn't a tangible thing as a lot of people think? What if the Christian belief of heaven is more of a symbolism than an actual thing.

As the discussion went further and this person began to think of heaven as the memories of lost loved ones and what they would expect, things turned quickly. The conversation became very positive and productive. This person now found value in heaven.

I have taken a similar path with someone as it relates to God. This person was not a firm believer and did not see value in God. I knew I could not force the issue, despite the fact that I have seen a ton of value in believing in God. Much like with heaven, I began with stating the value I get. I then started asking about the value they seek. They seemed to be very bitter about the world in general, but very obviously cared very deeply about those closest to them. We began talking very openly about the situation. Through that I said what if we just break down the typical Christian idea of God. Let's think of God as something bigger than us, anything bigger than us. As something that inspires, motivates, or guides us. What if God for you was just those people closest to you. Again, by focusing on the value and modifying things to bring that value we made some progress. Through this example this person has continued to grow and what they think of as God, has also continued to grow. This to me is continuous improvement!.

I now want to delve into something that I personally do outside of the church that came from the church utilizing lots of lean principles. During a sermon at one of the masses our priest was talking about light. In the Christian religions Jesus is considered the light. One thing he said jumped out to me very profoundly. He said light is amazing, it doesn't matter how many people consume it, it doesn't get reduced. Light is something that people follow. Light shines the same whether one person's consuming it or a million, sounds efficient right?

I started thinking very deeply about this from a Lean perspective. A key component of Lean is knowing what good looks like. And, not only knowing what good looks like but showing others what good looks like. If you think about that as it relates to Jesus being a light he is showing us what good looks like From a moral and ethical standpoint.

I started asking myself if I am a light? The answer I came up with is kind of. I was not alright with that and decided that my answer should be absolutely. In order to do that I had to understand what are those things that I wanted to be a light for. Through a lot of thought and reflection I developed a list. I have from time to time modified that list.

When I really think about what it means to be a light, I decided it is those behaviors that I want to display in a way that others see them and follow them. Maybe the best way to share this point is to share my current list of behaviors that I want to display in a way that others see them and follow them. The list is, work ethic, lean behavior, respect for people, passion, learn from the past, empower others, continuous improvement, giving for others, strong leadership, and thirst for learning.

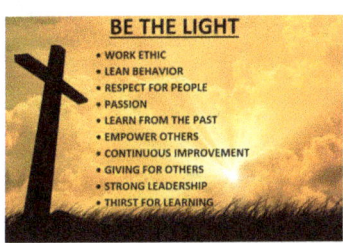

If you've read the earlier chapters you could guess I've created a visual for being a 'Light' and that visual exists on my Planner. I look at it every single day. There have been times where I am questioning my effectiveness as the light and when that happens I develop metrics around some or all of these and track them closely. Not only do I track them closely but I will set some goals around them if they need substantial improvement. I used the word substantial there because I am striving to continuously improve on those items every day, no matter what, as part of my continuous improvement lifestyle.

Another item I would like to share in this chapter comes from a Deacon I heard speak about heaven. Interestingly enough, after the mass I approached the Deacon to learn more about him. It turns out he is a retired software engineer that worked at a company that embraced Lean. He said in his sermon that life is a continuous improvement journey to get to heaven. We should all be looking to do better every day until the ultimate goal. You could imagine my brain was running at 1000 miles an hour and I wish I would have had a notepad at mass to take notes on the things he was saying. I was so excited to hear someone speaking so plainly about continuous improvement connecting to religion.

As I wrap this chapter up I firmly believe there is use for Lean continuous improvement in the actual facility of a church, that is pretty plain. I also believe there is a lot of personal impact if you analyze how you view religion from a System Aim standpoint utilizing continuous improvement, and understanding value.

LEAN IN THE
COMMUNITY

When you consider value and continuously improve to increase that value it would be hard for me to not want my community to be improving. This can be very challenging and a lot of what I'm going to speak to in this chapter is more aspirational than actual. I know someday I will have a bigger impact on the continuous improvement of our community but for now it's little bites.

When I think about improvement as it relates to community, I think it's important to define community. For me there is not just one definition. I have a community which is the people that live directly around me, our local community, I have a school community which is everyone within our school district, and even further the community of the entire Township.

If you start thinking about community and those different scopes and scales you can start thinking about what is the System Aim of that community and where are the gaps. Currently, I don't believe anyone of those has a defined System Aim. I will say within my community of those that live around me we all want to enjoy each other's company and help each other.

In order to do that there needs to be communication and understanding of what people need and where the gaps are. We currently do not have any formal system in place for this but I do make it a point during conversations to ask these questions about what people need and where I could be helping. I have several ideas in my head around how we can do a better job of formalizing all of this. We've talked several times about bringing everybody together for a picnic where we can put up some boards and talk about where there are gaps and where we all would like our neighborhood to be. I kind of wish we would have had that done before I started writing this book. I do think it will bring incredible value. Maybe you'll just have to buy a version two to find out?

Within the community of the school district things are a little more defined. There are certain things that we're all trying to achieve. Things such as funding the school district and improving sports programs. I have been plugging into these slightly, and need to do more. We've utilized lean continuous improvement to analyze the gaps on voting for certain needs. We have also discussed utilizing waste elimination to reduce the need for additional tax revenue. I'm constantly challenging the school community to be more transparent with goals and gaps. This has helped in certain areas, but still has a long way to go.

As far as a larger Township wide community, this is something that I aspire to take on and have done nothing with as of yet. I would love to see the broader community have a venue to get more engaged and voice ideas around what the community should look like, as well as where there are gaps. I don't think with the things on my list that I would ever want to be a politician, but I would certainly like to coach a politician through how to get this mentality ingrained in the community. I do plan to take some action and start to gently coerce some of the current politicians towards this way of thinking.

We did actually have a Congressman in our district that came from a Lean background and utilized Lean heavily during his term. I firmly believe his lack of reelection was due to voting of party lines as opposed to his actual effectiveness. I was incredibly impressed with him and he leveraged some amazing Lean tools to lead during his short time in office.

Every Sunday night he had a weekly huddle that would go out via email. In that huddle he would list what he did last week and what he's planning to do this week. If the things he did in the prior week were something that were recorded, he would provide links right there for you to watch it. If the things he was taking on or completed had some data associated with them, it would also be included in a link.

Another thing he did that impressed me was sending out voice of the customer surveys. As bigger issues were coming before him, he would e-mail out a survey. Some were one or two questions and some a lot more to get feedback from the masses. I do think the people that were in his political party were participating, but others weren't; that seems to be the state of our country right now. I still believe that if people would have taken it seriously and trusted him that he was operating with respecting all people and continuously improving not only would he still be there, but potentially other politicians would be looking at his model.

I again aspire to stick my nose into this and try and make things happen. I know there are others out there trying to get lean ingrained into political leaders that impact our community and I hope that comes to light someday.

I long for the day when all of those examples of community that I just gave have a transparent System Aim and a way

to communicate where the gaps are so that we are all collaboratively working towards that ideal state. Maybe even someday
all of those can filter up to a larger, grander, community of this
country, or even this world.

Lean — Let's Simplify

This chapter is an absolute necessity based on lessons I've learned over the years. One key thing I have learned on my lean journey is that I need to meet people where they are. Not everyone shares the passion for this that I have. In the past I have flooded people with my knowledge and my passion, just pushing it out there. In doing so I overwhelm them and they get nothing out of it. As I've just poured out so many of my thoughts around lean and so many different aspects of life, I feel I probably overwhelmed a lot of people.

I decided to plug in this chapter to help people understand that you don't need to do it all right away, or ever. This is continuous improvement. I strongly suggest starting at a level that you have a capacity for.

I want to remind everyone there are two key pillars. In Lean's most basic form just look at doing these two things; respecting people and continuously improving. If you are out there making things just a little bit better all the time, while respecting people you are utilizing Lean Continuous Improvement and you will see the value.

I want to break it down further into two other simple things that have a profound impact on this way of life. Those are System Aim and Key Behavior Indicators (KBI's). In the simplest form your System Aim is the ideal result and if you want to obtain an ideal result you have to display the ideal behaviors

When you think about Lean and improvement you have to think about what the data is telling you. If you have a System Aim, you should be able to measure how far away from it you are. If you then identify the behaviors that are required to achieve that System Aim, you should also be able to measure those; KBI's.

If you are uncertain where to get started or even if you are an expert but have never utilized KBI's I would encourage you to pick one area that you really want to focus on, establish a System Aim, list the behaviors that impact it and begin measuring them.

Lean Continuous Improvement is about increasing value; changing results for the better. If you want to change a result you need to change the behaviors that created the result. In order to change something in a productive, efficient, and no negative impact way you have to measure it.

All those words are saying is have a System Aim and utilize KBI's.

Simple and scalable, start small and take on bigger things as your journey progresses. I still find myself breaking things down into small chunks and trying to focus on progress and have been on this journey for a long time.

LEAN INTO EVERYTHING

The world is an amazing and complex place. Humans are an amazing and complex species. Humans and the world are also ripe for Lean Continuous Improvement. We as a world and species should be striving for the best!

We should all be on a Journey of Continuous Improvement towards a System Aim.

I mentioned earlier that this Chapter is very important to me and I encourage everyone to read it and more importantly act on it. This Chapter is not sharing of my journey and experience. This Chapter is aspirational and forward thinking.

When I think about how efficient Lean is at helping improve and fix problems in all the different areas I wrote about, I have to wonder why we are not utilizing this mentality to make improvements in the world. I mean hunger, poverty, oppression and violence are all more important that a Company's bottom line. Lean is being deployed broadly to improve those bottom lines. Why not deploy it to fix those bigger more important issues?

I fully understand there is no magic wand or silver bullet

that just fixes those things, but I am not talking about perfection here. I am talking about progress. I am talking about continuous progress that engages, empowers and respects people.

Let's start with a tough one that shouldn't be tough, **Politics.** This can be a touchy subject, especially in today's culture. It is very easy to align with a specific political party, maybe because your parents supported that party or maybe something went wrong for you and you blame the other party. Regardless of party I see a leadership gap. The current politicians are not collaboratively working, with data, to solve the biggest problems of the people. I would argue they don't even know the biggest problems of the people.

If you have experience with System Aim, or were able to develop some understanding of it from this book, could you imagine our politicians working with the people they are supposed to be representing to establish a System Aim? They are supposed to be Leaders and that is good leadership behavior!

Once that System Aim is established the leaders themselves or portions of their organization could be utilizing Gemba Walks to help understand and prioritize the biggest needs of the people.

I could also make a strong case for structured problem solving. Could you imagine if during their bid for office, or if a new piece of legislation is being passed that a problem statement was built? With that you would know with great detail, and more importantly data, what problem you are trying to solve, and what change you are trying to make. You would also be able to re-measure and see if your change has made the positive impact desired.

Wouldn't that be interesting? Politician Bob is seeking re-election and there is a definitive data set out there that shows very few of the problems that were attacked under his leadership got any better.

Another area I believe politics can benefit from Lean is Process Mapping. Wouldn't it be amazing if there was a visible, documented, continuously improving process that was shared to every voter on how you make your representative aware of the items you want to see improve. Within that process a mechanism to communicate progress and solicit thoughts on the Root Causes and Potential Countermeasures related to the issues.

I would imagine almost any Lean principle or tool can improve our political environment. And to be clear, by improve I mean all politicians become leaders and things are continuously getting better for the entire system; maybe someday the world/human race system. This would have to start small, someone would have to go first and show what good looks like. If you want to be first find me. I can help.

Now let's consider some more specific problem areas, **hunger and poverty**. When I think about money that is frivolously wasted and how much food finds a dumpster each day, then think about the elderly person that has to decide between heat or medication, or the kid picking though the trash so they don't starve to death. I can't help but think we can do better, much better and Lean can help.

Don't get me wrong, I am not much of a handout guy. I worked extremely hard to get where I am. I made lots of sacrifices. I watched lots and lots of people looking for handouts. They were relaxing with a beer and I was winding down a 20 hour day working two full time jobs, don't think for a minute that I am talking about giving everything away. A good Lean leader provides no solutions, they provide empowerment and engagement opportunities that result in improvements made by the people experiencing the struggles.

Again attacking these issues with structured problem

solving would really help. If you took a starving or impover-
ished area and started defining the issues with data, you could
then set some goals on the actual needs. Once that is defined
you could really start looking at the Root Cause of the problem, and with the people that are struggling where they are
struggling. Once those Root Causes are identified, some
potential countermeasures can be deployed.

I would place the countermeasures into two clearly
defined categories. The first being the ones the people in the
struggle are capable and empowered to put in place themselves. The second being the ones that they need outside help
for. I don't want to solution before the problem is defined, but
I can imagine there will be countermeasures in both
categories.

If you take that deeper and this is occurring in a portion of
a larger community, you can feed it all into a System Aim and
you will have resources available from a group that is all
rowing in the same direction.

I also think improvements in this area can be made if you
utilize some Lean tools like a KBI diagram or process map to
show what good looks like. If you have clear, data-based information about a similar area that is not having the same struggles, some simple best practice sharing can have a huge impact.

I also think this particular struggle can benefit greatly from
Visual Management. Visual Management of the identified
gaps, the desired behaviors and the progress or lack there of. I
would place these both in the struggling area and in any area
within the system that is not struggling as a motivation to
bring the entire system along.

I have to share something that happened to me just a
month ahead of writing this particular chapter. I was invited
to a leadership coaching event to present on Lean Leadership.
At that event were lots of amazing business owners, and also
some contributors like me. There was a lot of impactful

knowledge sharing and relationship building going on there. The one that I need to mention here is with a couple, Kathy and Beaver that are living this concept.

They do not have any formal Lean background or training. A lot of the terms I used and some of the ideas were very new to them. The interesting thing is that they are doing this. I could ramble on forever about what they are doing. I am so impressed by it. I will just share some real high-level stuff here and encourage you to go to their website

www.2ndstorygoods.com and buy Kathy's book, "Painfully Honest, the tale of a recovering helper."

This book details their journey of charity and support and how they learned that handing things out wasn't helping in the long run. She tells a powerful story about asking a poor starving Haitian woman what she has as opposed to what she needs. This turned into a thriving business that transformed the community and provides for hundreds. Their journey to change the world through this type of giving, opportunity not stuff, is growing and continuing today.

I simply had to mention them in this section, not only to help drum up support for them, but the correlation to Lean. When I present I read the room and adjust accordingly. I want to see energy and engagement, so I am constantly scanning and reading the room. I couldn't help but notice the focus she had on me while I was talking, as well as her feverishly taking notes. I was also extremely impressed with questions she was asking afterwards. I have to mention that I got a message from her about what she was doing with Lean on the plane ride home. That really warmed my heart. Every single time I train or speak I have a goal to inspire action. Here is action, and not only action but immediate action and by someone changing the world in ways that I hope to someday.

I also need to share that the last few Chapters of her book, she speaks a lot about the leader she has become and how that has changed so much over the years. As I was reading that section I lit up with excitement. As I journey around our company training and coaching potential Lean leaders I am trying to inspire them to do a lot of the things that Kathy ended up doing as a leader. As I read I was very impressed she is displaying Lean leadership behaviors and has never heard of Lean. She is doing it right.

I firmly believe that utilizing Lean Continuous Improvement in a more formal and intentional way can have a profound impact on decreasing poverty and hunger. Much like I said at the end of the political section, someone just needs to go first, someone kind of already has, so now let's get it to the next level. If you can make an impact and I can help, find me.

An emerging pain point that I think the world and the Human race really need to start applying Lean Continuous Improvement to is **Mental Health.** Our brains are being asked to evolve at an incredible rate right now. We are asking ourselves and our kids to process more information with their brain now, then ever before in history. With the explosion of social media platforms and other stimuli the problem is rapidly growing.

I can't help but think if some of the experts out there could develop a system aim and start utilizing structure problem solving, some progress could be made. I am sure this would be a heavy lift and would require incremental improvement.

I firmly believe a Lean approach to improving an issue like mental health, if it got the right subject matter experts behind it, started with in depth root cause analysis and accepted progress, made through collaboration and respecting people we could be moving in the right direction on this issue.

Now that I spoke to the broader problem and my thoughts on Lean helping, I want to talk about individuals that may be struggling. This can be difficult without help. If you are struggling there are lots of tips and suggestions in Chapter 7 that can have a very positive impact. Also, many studies have shown that physical health can have a huge positive or negative impact on mental health, so leveraging some tips from Chapter 8 to get yourself healthy would be a great step to take.

Some places I think Lean can really help an individual that is struggling with mental health are System Aim, Key Behavior Indicators (KBI's), Visual Management, structured problem solving and maybe even Poka Yoke (Mistake proofing).

First, getting a system aim will set a bit of a north star for you. It will allow you to really focus on where you want to be. Along your journey and your struggles this can help you to understand if things that are affecting you support your system aim or drive you away from it. Ideally, that would help you guide where your time is going, more time on items that support the system aim, less time on those that don't. Having metrics and visual management here would be helpful.

Next, KBI's, these can really help get ahead of things. I am no mental health expert, but I do know the earlier you can start making changes the easier it will be to get you back to feeling well. I am going to share a KBI system I use to improve my mental health. I start with a simple 1-5 ranking system for how I feel each day. With '1' being a really bad day and '5' being a really good day. At the end of each day I score myself.

Next, I listed out some of the things that happened, behaviors that make that number go down, the 'reds' and things that helped it go up, the 'greens'. After a period of time I have a pretty complete list of 'reds' and 'greens'. I could then start correlating those to the end result. For instance, if I had even 'red' and 'green' I was 1 or 2 for the day. I found that I needed more 'green' then 'red' to get to a '3' day and needed at least 3 'greens' to every 'red' to get a '5' day.

I used this data to help stay ahead of things. If I was experiencing a couple of 'reds' early in the day I knew I had to generate some 'greens' to even have a shot of a good day. What became interesting to me as I got more and more involved in this tracking system is that I recognized that most of the 'reds' were beyond my control, those things were happening to me no matter what. I also realized, almost every 'green' was within my control. I had ways to make them happen. I went as far as to block my calendar out for the afternoon with a note that said generate 'greens' on days that started with a plethora of 'reds'.

I do not use this tracking system anymore, as I feel I have a really good handle on when I need to start generating some 'greens', but if I get down in the dumps again and begin to struggle I will break it out again.

Sample of the KBI diagram:

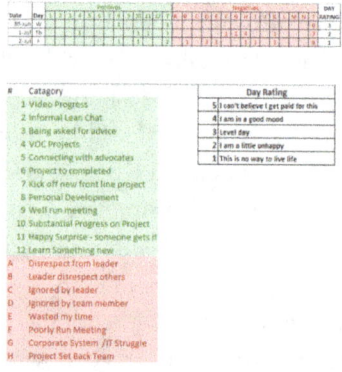

Utilizing visual management can be incredibly impactful. I gave lots of examples of visual management that drives desired behaviors earlier and all of those could be leveraged to aid in mental health. Visual Management should be simple, intuitive and most importantly drive the desired behaviors. If someone struggling can start to understand the desired behaviors they want as well as the behaviors they want to avoid, they can then sit down and try to develop visual management that helps.

I believe the above could really be aided by applying structured problem solving. If after a negative event the individual can sit down in a safe environment with a support team that respects them, they could run a structured problem-solving event. Possibly feeding any of the aforementioned tools. In a structured problem-solving event you identify, with data, the current state vs the desired state, your system aim can help here. The next step is to do the math and define the Gap, the difference between the two. You then set a target to close the Gap or a portion of the Gap. The next step is to conduct Root Cause Analysis. Define the thing or things that created the Gap. You then apply potential countermeasures, the thing or things that would eliminate the countermeasures. Next you define how the countermeasures will be implemented, this would include the support you might need. Finally after all of the countermeasures have been implemented you re-measure and confirm if you met your targets. If you have not, you start over with the new gap. The cycle continues until you achieve the results you wanted.

Lastly, I want to talk about mistake proofing or Poka Yoke. There are tons of examples of this in a manufacturing environment where defects can be engineered out of the process. I do think there could be some use on the mental health front. It would require someone much smarter than me to figure out

how to apply it. One example I might give is completely eliminating the ability for someone to access a social media platform. Let's say as an example someone's struggles are typically
being triggered by that media outlet. When that person is
feeling well, they may recognize that; the data would help, and
determine that is a root cause. I do think it is important that
they determine this. Once determined, they could take some
sort of measure to restrict themselves from ever having an
account or accessing the platform.

I by no means claim to be a mental health expert and have
an incredible amount of respect for those that are. I am also
not certain that field gets much exposure to a Lean way of
thinking. I felt strongly about writing this section just in case
they don't get exposure to this mindset and it could help. If
you are a mental health expert or know one, please share this.
If you are someone struggling or know someone struggling
share this.

I can help.

I want to wrap things up talking about where I think a
Lean Continuous Improvement mindset could help our
country and maybe our world to start closing the gap on
Racial Tensions.

There are so many Lean principles and tools that I think
can have a huge impact on improving Race relations. If you
look back to earlier in this chapter on politics, changing that
would be an improvement on this issue. I think a structured
problem-solving approach could be impactful. When I reflect
on what politics has done to try to improve these kind of
issues I feel like they are well intended, but most fall short. I
firmly believe that is because they are not able to get to the
Root Cause and apply countermeasures that eliminate those. I
also feel like too many political decisions on this front are
based on emotion and not data, so there is no confirmation if
the countermeasure are actually helping or hurting.

To me it seems pretty simple that a structured problem solving approach could help. What is not simple is how you actually do that at a scale that would be helpful. This is an area where I have some ideas, but would need lots of help. There are many highly influential people that could really help make a difference. If you happen to be one and you are reading this, reach out. I would love to share my thoughts.

If leaders were getting out to where a lot of this poor behavior rears it's ugly face and Gemba Walking I think more data driven root cause analysis could be done. There is a very specific way to Gemba Walk. Doing this wrong can have a massive negative impact. Doing it right can be the single most impactful thing you can do.

I would encourage people that want to do this to not only get properly trained, but also be coached until you are proficient. The key thing here is that you are not out there dispensing solutions, you are identifying empowerment Gaps and helping to close them. Imagine a time where leaders are out there clearly seeing and understanding where the people in their communities are not empowered to drive towards a system aim of Respecting Everyone and their sole purpose is to help close that Gap.

I am in no way thinking I have the magic wand or silver bullet to fix any of these problems, but I am thinking if more of the right people can start thinking and behaving this way there would be progress. I have seen Lean and Continuous Improvement positively impact absolutely everything I have applied it to. I have by far surpassed most expectations I have set for myself, all thanks to this mentality and I am far from done.

I am incredibly serious about leveraging what I have learned and I will continue to learn to make the world a better place. I have had some real success on this front in my current sphere of influence. I want to expand that sphere of influence and I need help. If this book has imparted some knowledge and inspired you and you want to be part of the mission to change the world by respecting people and continuously improving please move forward. If you want my help please find me. I care deeply about improvement, respecting people and making the world a better place. That is part of my personal mission statement.

————

My Mission Statement:

I will display a strong value for continuous improvement, leadership and developing others. I will leave a legacy of developing my family and at least 10 other families to behaviors of continuous improvement and respect for people.

Respect for others is fundamental. I mention a mere target of ten, this book will blow that out of the water. I need to set the bar higher for myself, continuously improve. Above all, if there's one enduring principle to carry forth from this book, it's this: Always uphold respect for people and commit to continuous improvement!

Sincerely,
Lucas J. Hahn

EPILOGUE

I want to highlight some thoughts from the book and share some insight on what's next. This is a continuous journey, so more will be coming.

I have struggled mightily in environments when I know this will help but it doesn't. I have learned, researched, analyzed and evaluated the root cause of that. It is always the culture. That is what most companies, teams and people miss about all of this. Our bad habits, aversion to change, profit first corporate cultures and fears have all put a leash on this otherwise successful endeavor.

I mentioned it already but can't say it enough, if you plan on getting on this journey you need to do this **with people, not to people**. Words like, empowerment, engagement, culture, inspiration, motivation, structure, leadership, and teamwork is the order of the day. These are things that need your focus and should be measured. You need to know where you stand on these and where there is opportunity to improve.

Part of my next phases of this journey is to help people develop a better understanding of what types of behaviors, the cultural components, put a leash on this motivating, empowering and valuable way of life. By understanding what leashes it we can generate a plan to unleash it.

The power of knowledge that can be leveraged for each and every one of you to unleash it begins in this book and will be fully in your hands and within your control soon. Stay Tuned!

Impactful Book List:

These are all great books that I would highly recommend and have really helped me out on my journey. I am not going to give a sales pitch on each one. This is the sale pitch for all of them. I will provide the Name, Author, and the general concept.

Leadership Reimagined, by Brian deFonteny – Lean focused book that challenges traditional command and control Management and gives examples of the good and the bad behaviors of those in leadership roles.

Lean-Driven Innovation, by Norbert Majerus – Lean focused book that documents the Lean journey of the R&D teams and Goodyear Tire and Rubber. This book identifies how an improvement culture can facilitate and inspire innovation.

The Machine That Changed the World, by James Womack – Lean focused book that gives a lot of the history, background and details of the Toyota Production System.

Awakening Your Ikegai, by Ken Mogi – Forward thinking self improvement book that explains the Okinawan philosophy. The reason you wake up everyday, your purpose.

2 Second Lean, by Paul Akers – Lean focused book that explains the unique and highly effective approach FastCap has taken to Lean.

Lean Health, by Paul Akers – A Lean Continuous Improvement approach to health. Provides lots of data and great examples of a Lean approach to health.

Be Unstoppable, by Alden Mills – A satirical story showing how to approach to goals and improvement written by an ex-Navy Seal that has an incredible amount of passion about improvement.

Unstoppable Teams, by Alden Mills – Building off his book Unstoppable, this dives deeper into the team dynamic and structure and focusses on the CARE loop to create unstoppable teams.

Getting Things Done, by David Allen – Book focused on efficiency, organization, prioritization and time management.

Creativity Inc., by Ed Catmull – This is what Good looks like for leadership. This documents the impact of sound, people first leadership behaviors at Pixar.

Start With Why, by Simon Sinek – I favor the live talks by Sinek over the books, he is one of the most engaging and dynamic presenters of our time. This book explains the importance of knowing Why. People will follow a solid Why.

The Infinite Game, by Simon Sinek – This book focusses on business culture and explains how poorly many businesses approach the idea of competition.

The Challenge Culture, by Nigel Travis – This book explains the importance of respectfully challenging things from all levels in a business culture. There is great perspective here as Nigel has experience with both Blockbuster Video and Dunkin Brands, one had it and one didn't.

Extreme Ownership, by Jocko Willink – like Sinek, the videos are really awesome, Jocko is incredibly motivating. The book focusses on not only leadership behaviors, but the behaviors of the entire team and how important ownership is.

Everybody Matters, by Bob Chapman – A book loaded with information on developing a people first business culture. Another great example of what good looks like from a CEO behavior standpoint.

Carrots and Sticks Don't Work, by Paul Marciano – This book is loaded with lots of information about reward and recognition and what motivates people and teams, as well as what demotivates them.

Who the Hell Wants to Work for You, by Tim Eisenhower – This book is loaded with lots of great examples of poor leadership behaviors and the negative impacts it can have on people and the business.

Culture Code, by Daniel Coyle – This culture focused book provides lots of keys and tips to develop an empowered and engaged culture. The importance of psychological safety is highlighted.

Fish, by Stephen Lundin – This fun and entertaining book shows the importance of mindset in a corporate culture and brings the culture of the famous Pike Place fish market in Seattle to the corporate world.

Legacy, by James Kerr – This culture and improvement focused book tells the story of the most successful professional sports franchise in the world, the New Zealand, All Blacks, Rugby Team.

Wandermust, by Mike Green – This exciting and entertaining book tells a great story, all while highlighting leadership behaviors and how to dig deep to develop them.

Painfully Honest, by Kathy Brooks – Incredible story about changing the world and some unintended consequences of charity if it is not done in a way that empowers people to succeed without the handouts.

The Tracks We Make, by Michael McGruther – This is a powerful, gripping story that is far too relatable to far too many people in withering, small, once prosperous towns in America. While it is a story it displays a journey of improvement and a constant seeking of value, to not be a Rust Belt statistic.

ADDITIONAL INFORMATION

For more information, question, comments, or suggestions:
Lucashahn9@gmail.com

www.LeanUnleashed.com